Level A
Contents

BASIC Phonics Skills

Basic Phonics Skills
What's in Level A?

Emergent Skills Practice

Choose from a number of reproducibles to strengthen readiness skills.

- left–right
- top–bottom
- same–different
- beginning–middle–end
- print awareness

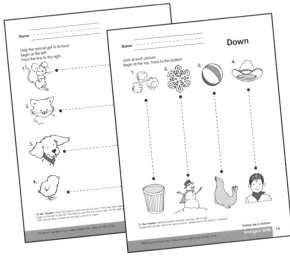

Phonemic Awareness Practice

Skill sheets present varying levels of difficulty to meet individual student needs.

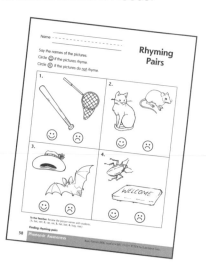

easiest ←——————→ more difficult

Basic Phonics Skills, Level A • EMC 3318 • ©2004 by Evan-Moor Corp.

Alphabetic Awareness Practice

Reproducibles provide practice in forming the letters of the alphabet. Activity sheets are in both traditional and modern versions.

traditional

modern

Sound-Symbol Association Practice

Reproducibles provide a range of practice for each letter of the alphabet. There will be an activity to fit each student's needs.

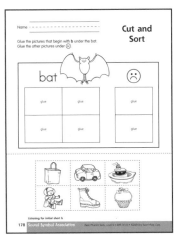

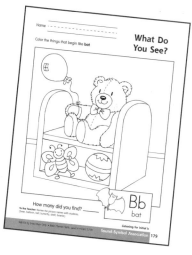

easiest ←————————————————————→ more difficult

Little Alphabet Readers

Reproducible storybooks for each letter of the alphabet. Just reproduce, cut out, fold, and use.

Tracking Student Progress

Use the form on page 5 to record the progress of each student. The rubric provided below will help you assess each student's level of competence. Students who fail to achieve a 2 or 3 level should be provided additional instruction and practice until they become proficient.

Mastered **3**	• The student is able to complete the activity independently. • The student is able to complete the activity correctly. • The student is able to answer questions about the phonetic principle being practiced.
Showed Adequate Understanding **2**	• The student is able to complete the activity with little assistance. • The student is able to complete the activity with minimal errors. • The student is able to answer questions about the phonetic principle being practiced.
Showed Inconsistent Understanding **1**	• The student required assistance to complete the activity. • The student made several errors. • The student did not appear to understand the phonetic principle being practiced.
Showed Little or No Understanding **0**	• The student required one-to-one assistance to complete the activity. • The student made many errors. • The student showed no understanding of the phonetic principle being practiced.

Basic Phonics Skills, Level A • EMC 3318 • ©2004 by Evan-Moor Corp.

Basic Phonics Skills, Level A
Student Record Form

Name _____

Sound or Skill Practiced	Level A Page Number	Date Completed	3 Mastered	2 Showed Adequate Understanding	1 Showed Inconsistent Understanding	0 Showed Little or No Understanding

The Benefits of Phonics Instruction

Words are made of letters, and letters stand for sounds. That is the simple basis for providing phonics instruction to all beginning readers. Research has shown that all children will benefit from being taught the sound-spelling connection of the English language (Chall, 1967). Phonics instruction leads to decoding, which gives beginning readers one more strategy to use when faced with an unfamiliar word.

Research has shown the following to be true:

- Strong decoding skills in early readers correlate highly with future success in reading comprehension (Beck and Juel, 1995).
- As more and more "sounded-out" words become sight words, readers have more time to devote to the real reason for reading: making meaning from print (LaBerge and Samuels, 1974; Freedman and Calfee, 1984).
- Readers who are good decoders read more words than those who are poor decoders (Juel, 1988).
- Children with limited learning opportunities and abilities benefit most from phonics instruction, but more able children also benefit (Chall, 1967).
- Those who are successful decoders do not depend on context clues as much as those who are poor decoders (Gough and Juel, 1991).

The best readers can decode words. As a result, those readers grow in word recognition, fluency, automaticity, and comprehension. "Sounding out" unfamiliar words is a skill that benefits all readers. These new words quickly become "sight words," those recognized immediately in text, which allow the reader to spend more time on new words. This cycle is the foundation that creates reading success, and successful readers are better learners.

BASIC Phonics Skills

Basic Phonics Skills, Level A • EMC 3318 • ©2004 by Evan-Moor Corp.

Emergent Skills

Look!

Look at each sign.
Circle any words. Tell about the signs.

1.

2.

3.

4.

5.

6.

To the Teacher: Discuss what each sign means and where we see it.

Recognizing environmental print

Look at each picture.
Tell what it means.
Tell where you see each one.
Draw a line to match the pairs.

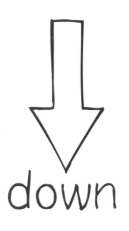

To the Teacher: Discuss how each sign helps us.
Ask students to circle any words they see on the signs.

Recognizing and matching environmental print

Name _____

Left and Right

Look at the hands.
Trace the left hand yellow.
Trace the right hand red.

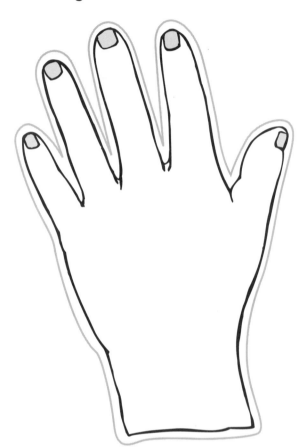
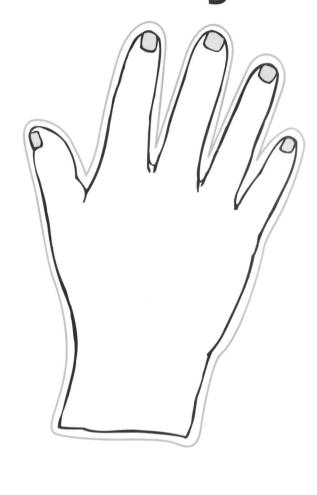

Circle the left.	**Circle the right.**

To the Teacher: Have students place their hands on the hands pictured here. Practice removing the left and then the right. Involve students in using the terms *left* and *right* and identifying the hand that matches. Invite them to add rings or other details to the illustration.

Distinguishing left and right

Yum!

Help the animal get to its food.
Begin at the left.
Trace the line to the right.

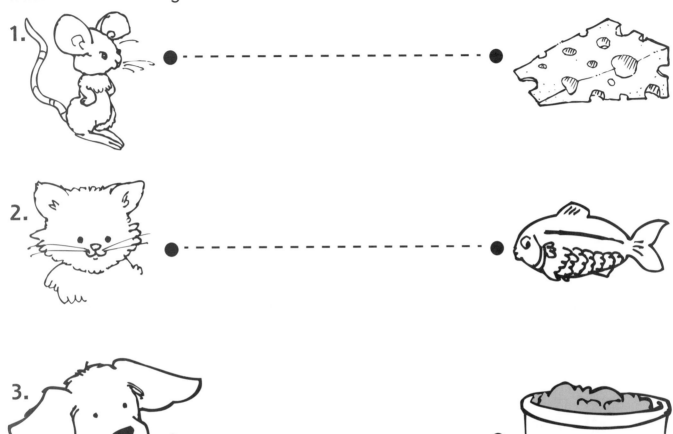

To the Teacher: Have students name the picture pairs. Then have them place their index finger on the dot on the left. Tell them to trace the line to the right. Do this with all four. Then instruct them to draw the line with a pencil or crayon.

Tracing left to right

Name _____

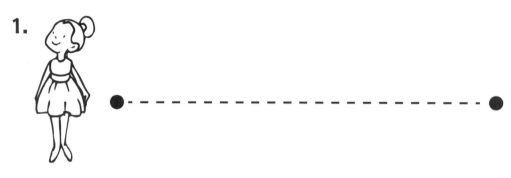

Shoes

Help each girl find her shoes.
Begin at the left.
Trace the line to the right.

1.  •- - - - - - - - - - - -•

2.  •- - - - - - - - - - - -•

3.  •- - - - - - - - - - - -•

4. •- - - - - - - - - - - -•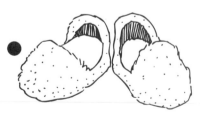

To the Teacher: Trace with fingers from left to right before doing the activity with a pencil or crayon.
Tell students that we read from left to right. Demonstrate with a short sentence on the chalkboard.
Model the fact that we also write from left to right.

Tracing left to right

Top and Bottom

Look at each picture.
Color the top thing red.
Color the bottom thing blue.

1.

2.

3.

4.

To the Teacher: Involve students in naming each object on the page.
Ask them to identify which part of the picture is on the top and which is on the bottom.
Encourage them to answer in complete sentences.

Distinguishing top and bottom

Emergent Skills   13

Connect

Look at each picture.
Begin at the top. Trace to the bottom.

1. 2. 3. 4.

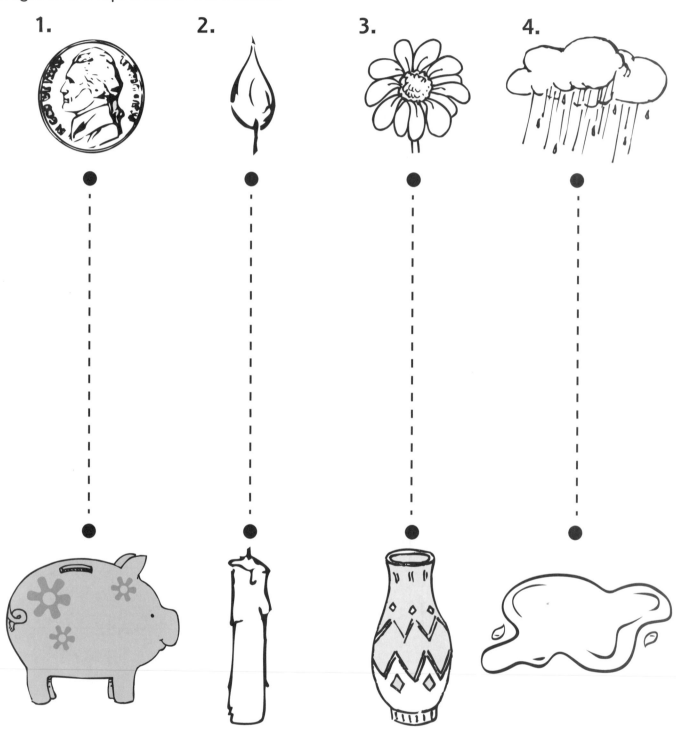

To the Teacher: Have students identify each pair of objects. Begin by having them trace the line with their finger from top to bottom. Then instruct them to draw the line with a pencil or crayon.

Tracing top to bottom

Down

Look at each picture.
Begin at the top. Trace to the bottom.

1.   2.   3.   4.

To the Teacher: Remind students that we read from left to right.
Explain that we also read from top to bottom. Model this on the chalkboard or overhead.

Tracing top to bottom

Name

Same or Different?

Look at each pair.
Color the pair if both are the same.

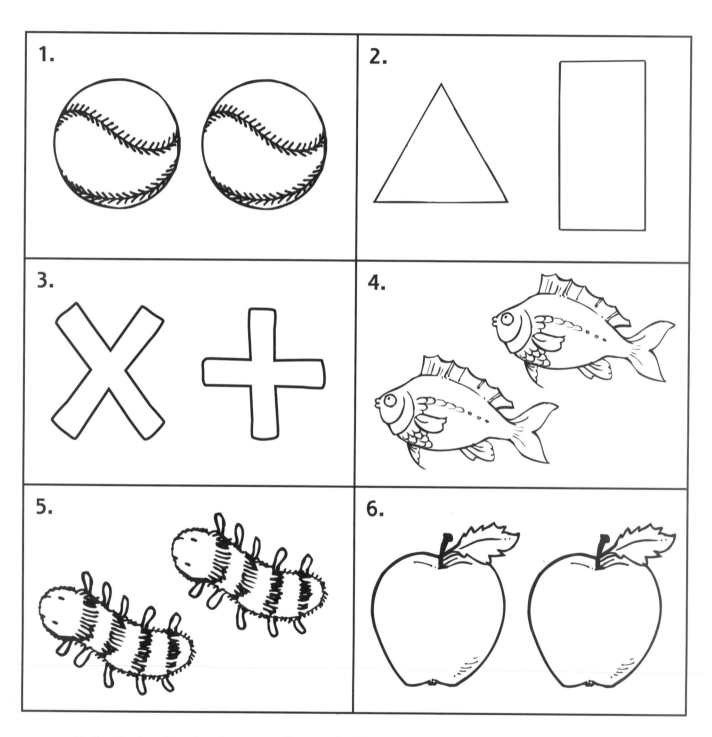

To the Teacher: Introduce the concept of same and different. Use pairs of items in the classroom to demonstrate the concepts. Encourage students to verbalize their observations. As the children work on this page, remind them to work from left to right, top to bottom.

Choosing objects that are the same

Party Time

Look at each pair.
Color the pair if both pictures are the same.

To the Teacher: Have two students stand in front of the class.
Ask the class to tell how the two are the same.

Choosing objects that are the same

Emergent Skills 17

Name

Many Cars

Look carefully.
Draw a line from left to right to connect the ones that are the same.

1.

2.

3.

4.

To the Teacher: Ask students to name the items that are the same on all of the cars. (wheels, windows, facing same direction, etc.)

Matching objects that are the same

Basic Phonics Skills, Level A • EMC 3318 • ©2004 by Evan-Moor Corp.

Draw a line to connect the leaves that are the same.

1.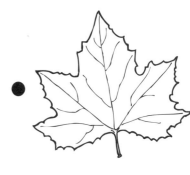

2.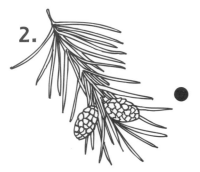

3.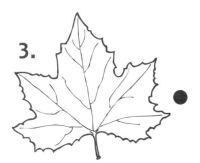

4.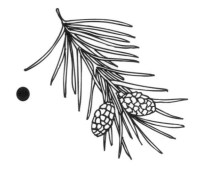

To the Teacher: Remind students that we work from left to right and top to bottom. Have students trace with their fingers before they do the job with a crayon or pencil.

Matching objects that are the same

Trace and Draw

Look at the shape on the left.
Trace and draw the same shape again.

1.

2.

3.

4.

To the Teacher: Ask students, "Where is the triangle?" "Where is the rectangle?" "Where is the circle?"
"Where is the square?" Ask them to compare a square and a triangle.

Drawing objects that are the same

Look at Shapes

Color the one that matches the first one.

1.

2.

3.

4.

To the Teacher: Review with students the names of the shapes.
Encourage them to look around the room for objects that match those shapes.
Make students aware of these shapes and their basic characteristics.

Identifying objects that are the same

Name

Same or Different?

Color the one that is different in each row.

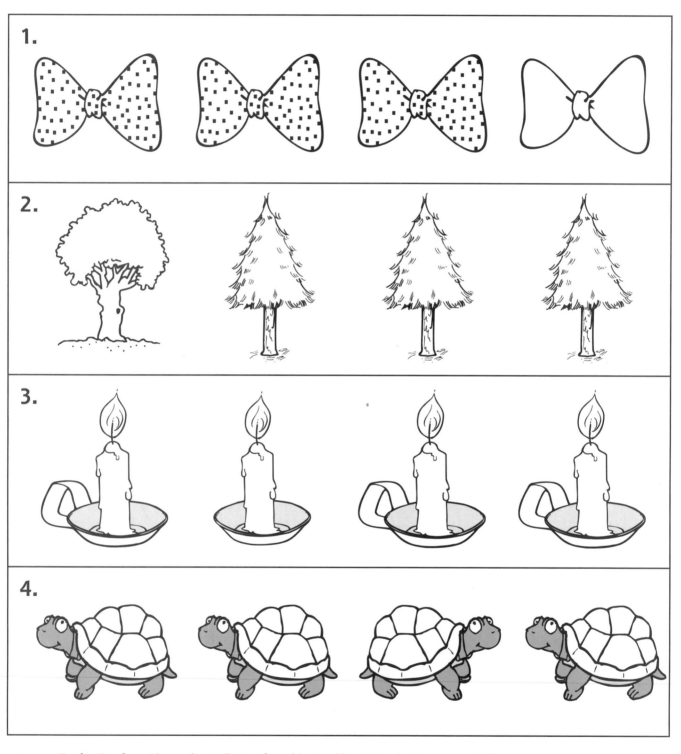

To the Teacher: Discuss the attributes of an object and how it can be the same or different.
Explain that "different" can mean many things: different sizes, images, missing parts, facing another direction, etc.
Encourage students to explain how each item they choose is different and what makes the other items "the same."

Choosing objects that are different

Which One?

Color the one that is different in each row.
Tell why it is different.

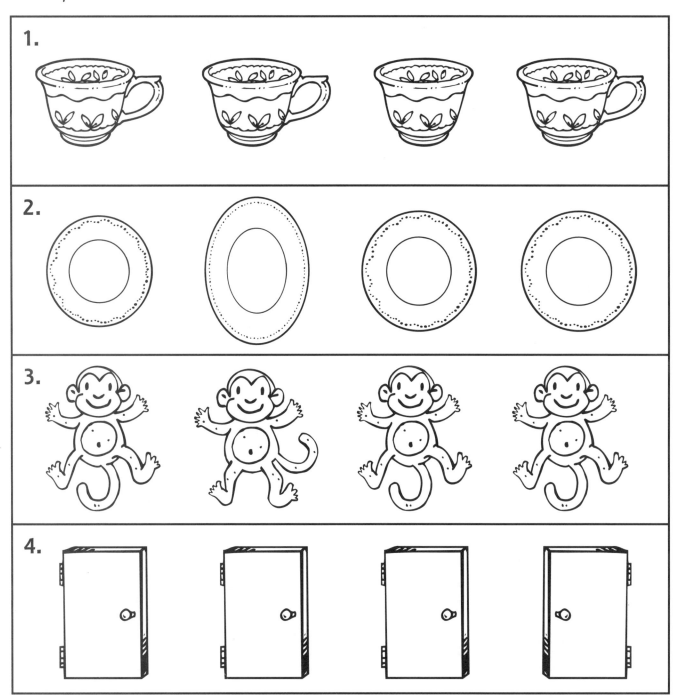

1.

2.

3.

4.

To the Teacher: Review each item on the worksheet with students.
Discuss what makes one item different and the others fit in the category of "the same."

Distinguishing between objects

Name

Look at each pair.
Draw the missing part.

To the Teacher: Develop visual awareness of what makes a pair of objects the same or different in some way. Discuss each pair and what would need to be done to make both objects the same.

Distinguishing differences

Look for the Same

Circle the ones that match the first one.

1.	a	a	a	d	a
2.	b	b	h	b	b
3.	r	n	r	r	r
4.	t	t	t	l	t
5.	c	c	a	c	c
6.	d	d	b	d	d

To the Teacher: Focus on the characteristics of letters.
Discuss with students what makes some of the letters different.

Distinguishing letters

Emergent Skills   25

Name

Just Alike

Look at each pair of pictures.
Add the missing part to make the pictures match.

To the Teacher: Ask students to name what is different in each pair of pictures. Encourage them to respond in complete sentences. When the task is complete, ask students to circle any letters or words that appear as a part of the pictures.

Adding the missing part

Name

Color the one at the beginning of each row.

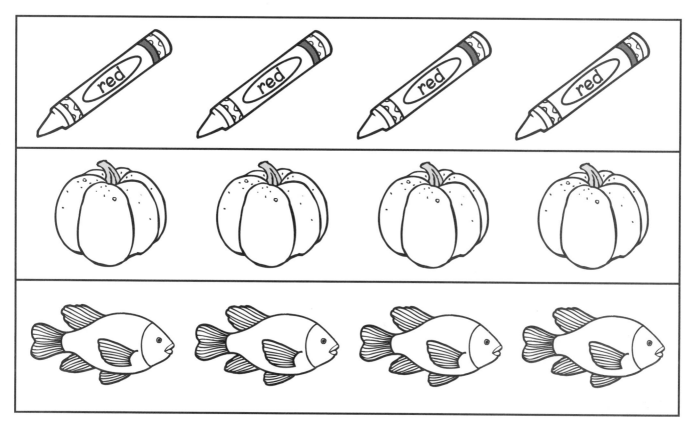

Draw one at the beginning of each row.

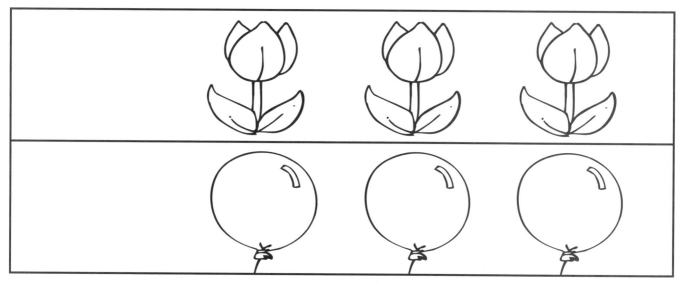

To the Teacher: Remind students that we read by beginning on the left.
Ask students to put their index finger on the beginning picture of each row.

Recognizing the beginning

At the End

Color the picture that is at the end of the row.
Circle the picture at the beginning.

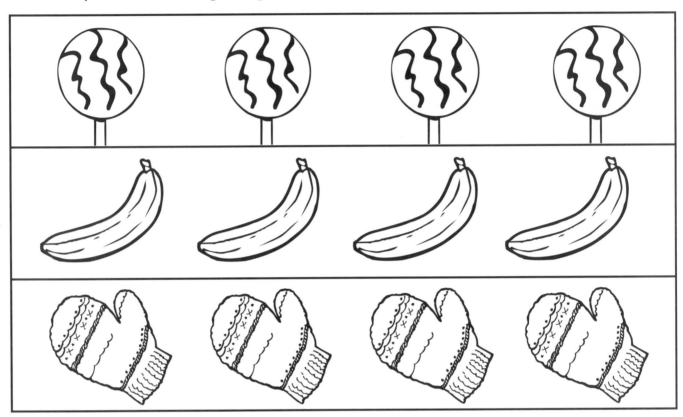

Draw one at the end of each row.

To the Teacher: Remind students that we read from left to right. Ask students to touch each item in the row, identifying what they are doing: "I am beginning on the left and moving to the end (right)."

Recognizing the beginning and end

In the Middle

Color the picture that is in the middle of the row.
Circle the one at the beginning. Cross out the one at the end.

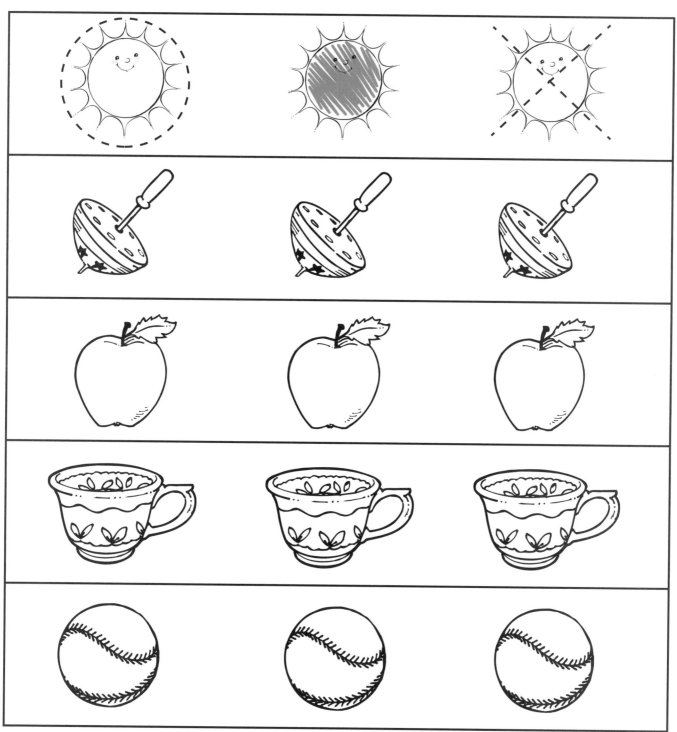

To the Teacher: Ask three students to stand in front of the class. Do activities that reinforce for students which student is in the middle, at the beginning, and at the end.

Recognizing the beginning, middle, and end

Name _____

Beginning, Middle, or End?

Which one is missing?
Draw the missing picture.
Tell if it is beginning, middle, or end.

1.

2.

3.

4.

To the Teacher: Ask students to say which picture in each row is missing.

Recognizing the beginning, middle, and end

Emergent Skills   Basic Phonics Skills, Level A • EMC 3318 • ©2004 by Evan-Moor Corp.

Name -

Where?

Look at the objects in the box. Find those hidden objects
in the picture. Circle the hidden objects.

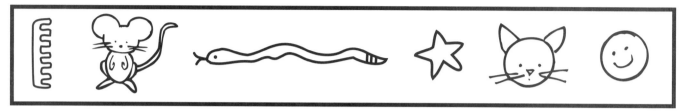

To the Teacher: Develop positional words by having students describe where they find each object.
(under the chair, on the bookshelf, by the desk, etc.)

Finding hidden pictures

Name _____

The Picnic

Look at the objects in the box. Find those hidden
objects in the picture. Circle the hidden objects.

To the Teacher: Develop visual skills by having students search for hidden objects.

Finding hidden pictures

Basic Phonics Skills, Level A • EMC 3318 • ©2004 by Evan-Moor Corp.

Name _____

Look at the letters in the box. Find those hidden letters in the picture. Circle the hidden letters.

M	F	P	C	X

To the Teacher: Students focus on the characteristics of capital letters as they search for them hidden in a picture. Encourage discussion of where the letters are found, emphasizing words that describe location: *above, below, beside, on, under,* etc.

Finding hidden pictures

Name

Under the Sea

Look at the letters in the box. Find those hidden letters in the picture. Circle the hidden letters.

s	g	m	f	w

To the Teacher: Students focus on the characteristics of lowercase letters as they search for them hidden in a picture. Encourage discussion of where the letters are found, emphasizing words that describe location: *above*, *below*, *beside*, *on*, *under*, etc.

Finding hidden pictures

Basic Phonics Skills, Level A • EMC 3318 • ©2004 by Evan-Moor Corp.

Name -

Which Way?

Look at the pictures in each row.
Circle the picture that faces a different way.

To the Teacher: Review left and right, same and different.
Apply those concepts as you model finding the reversed picture in the first row.

Choosing the reversed object

Emergent Skills

Name

Wrong Turn!

Look at the pictures in each row.
Circle the picture that faces a different way.

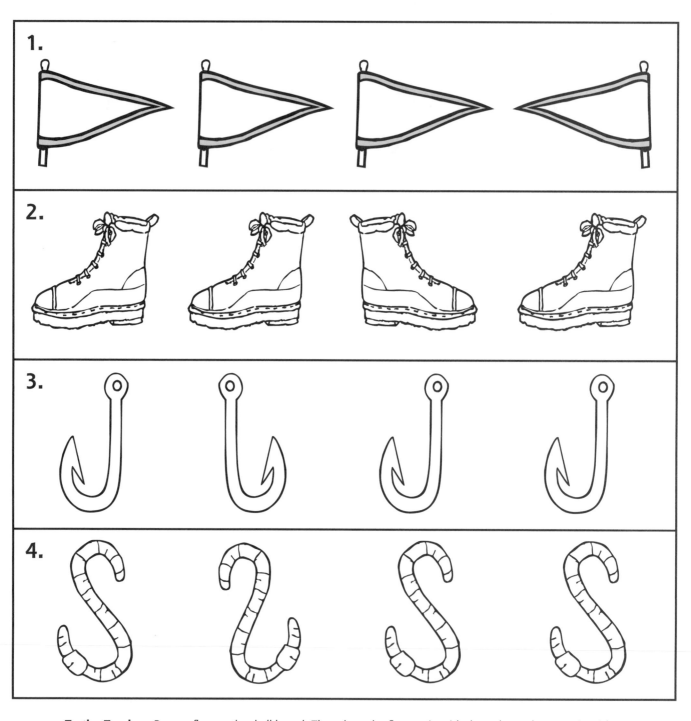

To the Teacher: Draw a flag on the chalkboard. Then draw the flag again with the pole on the opposite side.
Explain that the second one faces in a different direction. Look at a side view of a chair in the classroom.
Turn it the other way and discuss what has changed. Encourage students to verbalize what is different.

Choosing the reversed object

What's Wrong?

Circle the six things that are wrong in this picture.
Check off each one.

✓___1 ___2 ___3 ___4 ___5 ___6

To the Teacher: Explain that good readers can tell when something is wrong by how it looks.
Ask students to identify and explain one thing in the picture that is wrong.

Identifying what is wrong in a picture

Name _____

Think About It

Circle the things that are wrong in this picture.

To the Teacher: Teach students to evaluate a scene for inconsistencies.

Identifying what is wrong in a picture

Emergent Skills

Basic Phonics Skills, Level A • EMC 3318 • ©2004 by Evan-Moor Corp.

Go Together

Look at the first picture in each row.
Look at each of the other pictures in that row.
Color the two that go with the first picture.

To the Teacher: Name 3 things that go together, such as pie, cake, and ice cream. Ask students what category all of these fit into. (desserts, sweets) Repeat this activity to encourage students to think about categories of objects.

Identifying objects that go together

Two of a Kind

Look at each pair of pictures.
Circle each pair that goes together.

To the Teacher: Ask students to tell how the object pairs are related.
More than one answer may apply.

Identifying objects that go together

Name _____

A Good Match

Draw a line to connect the pairs that go together.

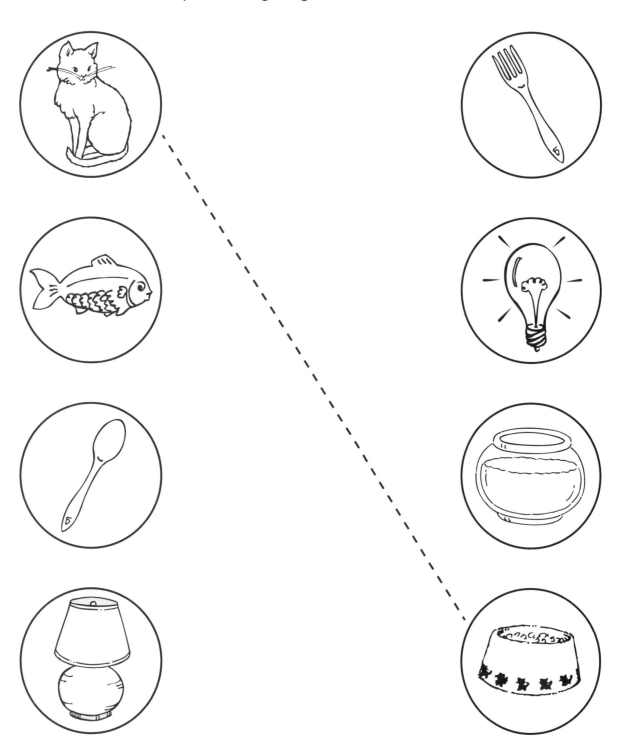

To the Teacher: Ask students to explain their reasons for pairing objects together.

Matching objects that go together

Match the Pairs

Draw a line to connect the pairs that go together.

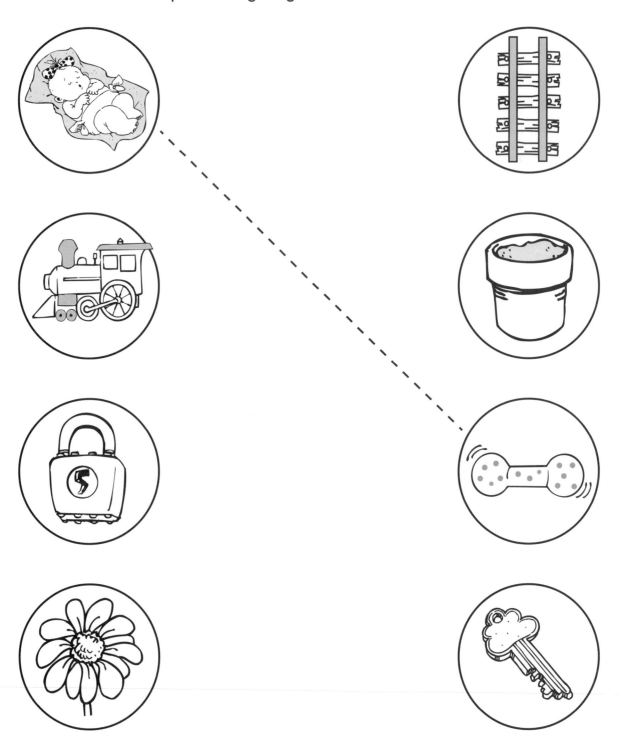

To the Teacher: Ask students to explain their reasons for pairing objects together.

Matching objects that go together

Name

Make an **X** on the picture in each row that does <u>not</u> belong.

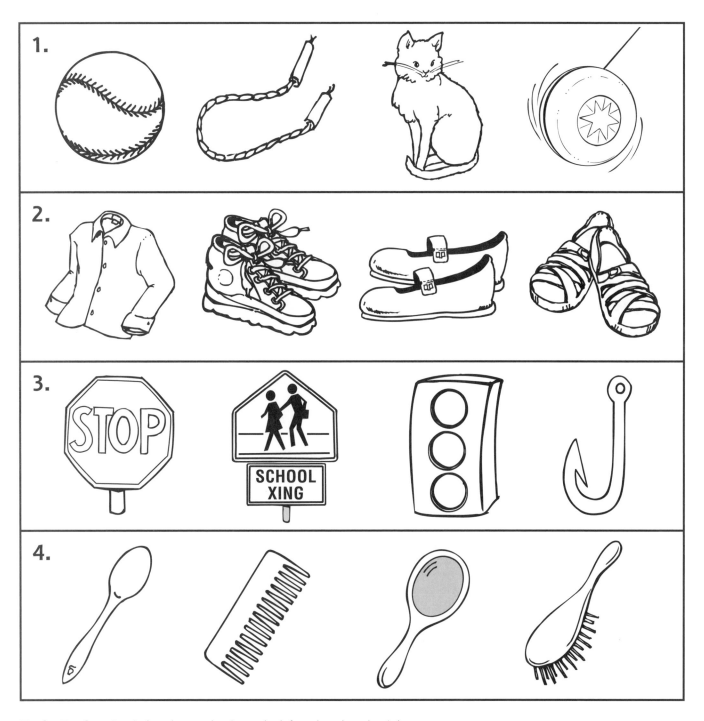

To the Teacher: Remind students to begin on the left and work to the right. Discuss which objects belong and which do not. Ask them to name the category or group name for each row. (toys, shoes, grooming objects, etc.)

Choosing the object that does not belong

Emergent Skills

Name

X It Out

Color the pictures in each row that go together.
Make an **X** on the one that does <u>not</u> belong.

To the Teacher: Remind students to begin on the left and work to the right.
Discuss which objects belong and which do not. Ask them to name the category
or group name for each row. (objects in space, animals, tools, etc.)

Choosing the object that does not belong

Name _____

Draw One More

Draw a picture of something that goes in each of the groups.

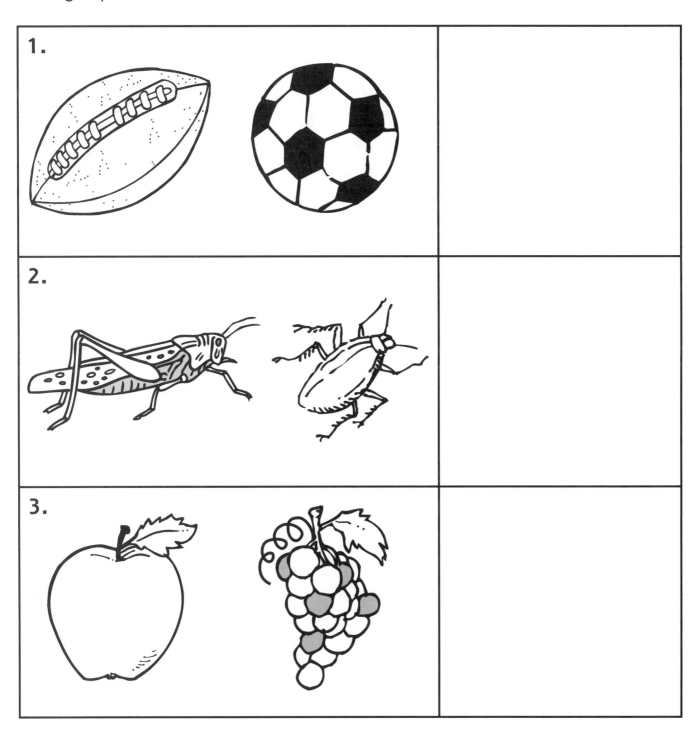

To the Teacher: Ask students to name the category or group name for each row. (sports balls, bugs, fruits, etc.)

Adding an object that belongs

Name _____

Word Time!

Words are made of letters.
Circle the words in this picture.

To the Teacher: Explain that words are made of letters. In the real world, we see words everywhere. Encourage students to look around them and find words in their world.

Distinguishing words from pictures

Phonemic Awareness

©2004 by Evan-Moor Corp. • Basic Phonics Skills, Level A • EMC 3318

Name ----------

Words have parts. Listen and count.

To the Teacher: Review the picture names with students.
(apple, star, fish, table, baby, house)

Counting 1- & 2-syllable words

Name _____

3 in a Row

Say the name of the picture. Clap the parts.
O the ones with 1 clap.
X the ones with 2 claps.
Look for 3 in a row.

To the Teacher: Review the picture names with students.
(cookie, hat, fork, cup, table, shoe, apple, clock, button)

Counting 1- & 2-syllable words

Count Them

Say the name of the picture. Clap the parts.
Write **1** for one clap.
Write **2** for two claps.

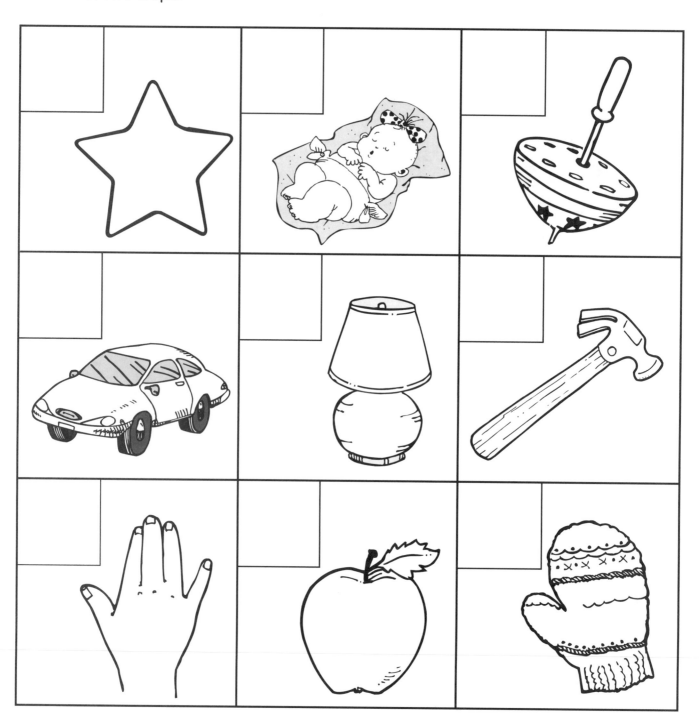

To the Teacher: Review the picture names with students.
(star, baby, top, car, lamp, hammer, hand, apple, mitten)

Counting 1- & 2-syllable words

Clap and Count

Say the name and clap.
Glue the pictures under the number of claps you hear.

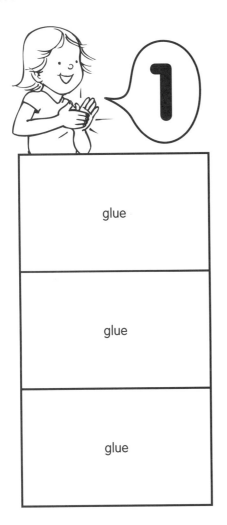

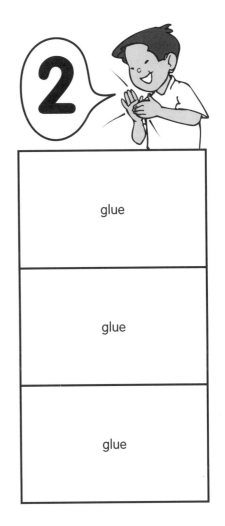

Counting 1- & 2-syllable words

Phonemic Awareness

Name

Say the name of each picture.
Clap to count the parts.
Circle the number.

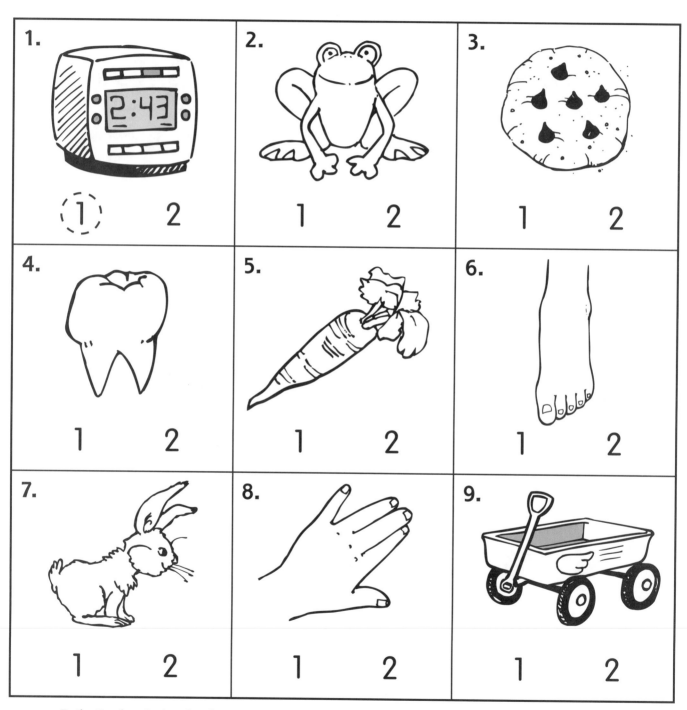

1. ① 2

2. 1 2

3. 1 2

4. 1 2

5. 1 2

6. 1 2

7. 1 2

8. 1 2

9. 1 2

To the Teacher: Review the picture names with students.
(clock, frog, cookie, tooth, carrot, foot, rabbit, hand, wagon)

Counting 1- & 2-syllable words

Say the name and clap.
Glue the pictures under the
number of claps you hear.

glue	glue	glue
glue	glue	glue

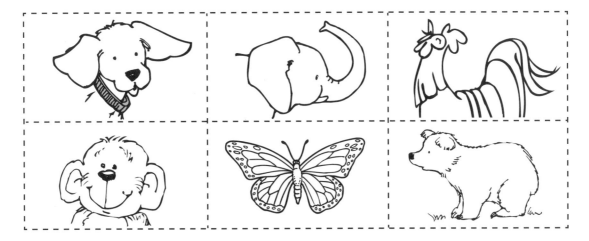

Counting 1-, 2-, & 3-syllable words

Listen for the Claps

Say the name of each picture.
Clap to count the parts.
Circle the number.

1. 1 2 3

2. 1 2 3

3. 1 2 3

4. 1 2 3

5. 1 2 3

6. 1 2 3

7. 1 2 3

8. 1 2 3

9. 1 2 3

To the Teacher: Review the picture names with students.
(bird, elephant, mug, basket, butterfly, lettuce, hat, hamster, ladybug)

Counting 1-, 2-, & 3-syllable words

Name

Say the name of each picture.
Clap to count the parts.
Draw a line to show how many syllables you hear.

To the Teacher: Review the picture names with students.
(hand, butterfly, rabbit, frog, elephant, ladybug, wagon, lettuce)

Counting 1-, 2-, & 3-syllable words

Phonemic Awareness   55

Name _____

Color the picture if it rhymes with **cat**.

Fat Cat

WELCOME

To the Teacher: Review the picture names with students.
(dog, hat, heart, bat, rat, mat)

Identifying words that rhyme

Basic Phonics Skills, Level A • EMC 3318 • ©2004 by Evan-Moor Corp.

Name _____

Find the Rhyme

I see a cat
that is so fat.

Circle the pictures in each row that rhyme.

1.

2.

3.

To the Teacher: Review the picture names with students.
(**1.** cat, dog, hat; **2.** hat, mat, bat; **3.** bat, net, rat)

Distinguishing rhyming words

Name _____

Say the names of the pictures.

Circle 😊 if the pictures rhyme.

Circle ☹ if the pictures do <u>not</u> rhyme.

To the Teacher: Review the picture names with students.
(**1.** bat, net; **2.** cat, rat; **3.** hat, bat; **4.** bug, mat)

Finding rhyming pairs

Color the picture if it rhymes with **cake**.

Cake Bake

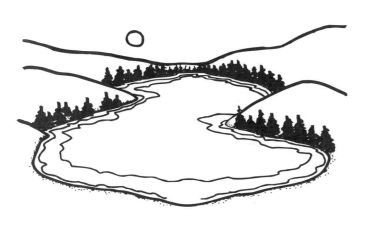

To the Teacher: Review the picture names with students.
(rain, rake, flake, sack, lake, snake)

Identifying words that rhyme

Find the Rhyme

I can bake
a big, big cake.

Circle the pictures in each row that rhyme.

1.

  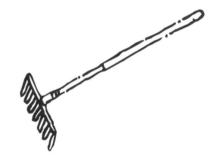

2.

3.

To the Teacher: Review the picture names with students.
(**1.** steak, grapes, rake; **2.** shake, snake, boat; **3.** flake, cap, lake)

Distinguishing rhyming words

Name

Rhyming Pairs

Say the names of the pictures.

Circle ☺ if the pictures rhyme.

Circle ☹ if the pictures do <u>not</u> rhyme.

To the Teacher: Review the picture names with students.
(**1.** rake, snake; **2.** tape, lake; **3.** shake, flake; **4.** cake, grapes)

Finding rhyming pairs

Name _____

Say the name of each picture.
Glue them in sets that rhyme.

glue	glue
glue	glue
glue	glue

Identifying words that rhyme

Basic Phonics Skills, Level A • EMC 3318 • ©2004 by Evan-Moor Corp.

Color the picture if it rhymes with **ship**.

Sounds Like Ship

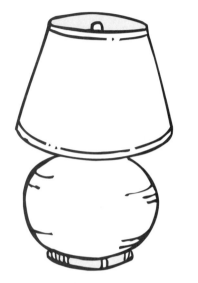

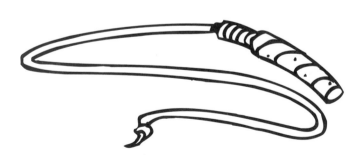

To the Teacher: Review the picture names with students.
(lamp, pin, pup, lip, whip, rip)

Identifying words that rhyme

Find the Rhyme

Circle the pictures in each row that rhyme.

1.

2.

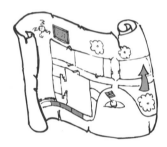 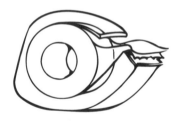 

3.

  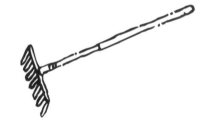

4.

To the Teacher: Review the picture names with students.
(**1.** lip, cap, rip; **2.** map, ship, drip; **3.** cake, tape, rake; **4.** hat, bat, lamp)

Distinguishing rhyming words

Name _____

Rhyming Pairs

Say the names of the pictures.

Circle 😊 if the pictures rhyme.

Circle 🙁 if the pictures do <u>not</u> rhyme.

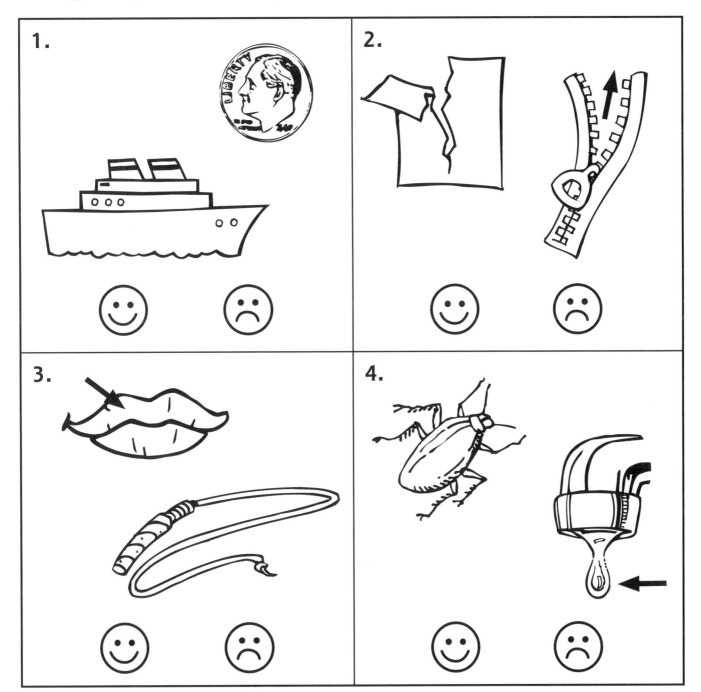

To the Teacher: Review the picture names with students.
(**1.** ship, dime; **2.** rip, zip; **3.** lip, whip; **4.** bug, drip)

Finding rhyming pairs

Color the picture if it rhymes with **kite**.

Kite Time

To the Teacher: Review the picture names with students.
(bike, light, dime, bite, write, night)

Identifying words that rhyme

Find the Rhyme

Circle the pictures in each row that rhyme.

1.

2.

3.

4.

To the Teacher: Review the picture names with students.
(**1.** pin, knight, light; **2.** bite, shoe, night; **3.** lip, kite, ship; **4.** rake, rat, snake)

Distinguishing rhyming words

Name _____

Rhyming Pairs

Say the names of the pictures.

Circle 😊 if the pictures rhyme.

Circle 😞 if the pictures do <u>not</u> rhyme.

To the Teacher: Review the picture names with students.
(**1.** kite, light; **2.** bite, bike; **3.** ship, rip; **4.** cat, rat)

Finding rhyming pairs

Ship or Kite?

Say the name of each picture.
Glue them in sets that rhyme.

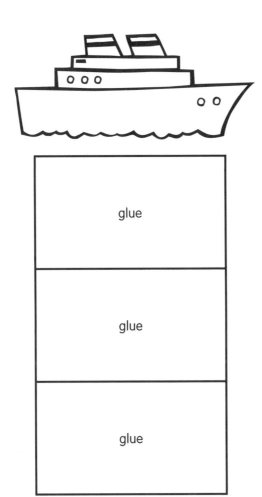

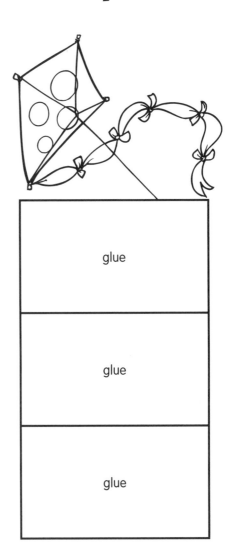

glue
glue
glue

glue
glue
glue

Identifying words that rhyme

Color the picture if it rhymes with **goat.**

Go, Goat

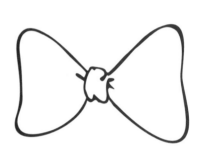

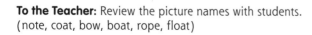

To the Teacher: Review the picture names with students.
(note, coat, bow, boat, rope, float)

Identifying words that rhyme

Find the Rhyme

Circle the pictures in each row that rhyme.

1.

2.

  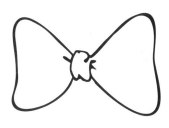

3.

4.

To the Teacher: Review the picture names with students.
(**1.** comb, goat, note; **2.** boat, rope, float; **3.** cake, lake, bow; **4.** lip, night, light)

Distinguishing rhyming words

Rhyming Pairs

Say the names of the pictures.

Circle ☺ if the pictures rhyme.

Circle ☹ if the pictures do <u>not</u> rhyme.

To the Teacher: Review the picture names with students.
(**1.** float, rope; **2.** note, bow; **3.** goat, soap; **4.** coat, boat)

Finding rhyming pairs

Color the picture if it rhymes with **top**.

The Top

To the Teacher: Review the picture names with students. (soap, mop, dog, stop, hop, sock)

Find the Rhymes

Circle the pictures in each row that rhyme.

1.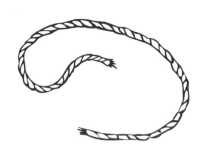

2.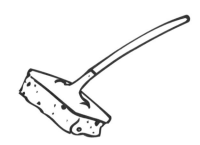

3.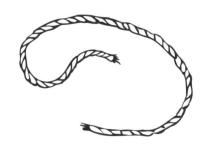

4.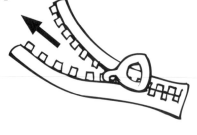

To the Teacher: Review the picture names with students.
(**1.** top, rope, hop; **2.** sock, mop, pop; **3.** stop, soap, rope; **4.** zip, pin, ship)

Distinguishing rhyming words

74 **Phonemic Awareness**

Name

Rhyming Pairs

Say the names of the pictures.

Circle ☺ if the pictures rhyme.

Circle ☹ if the pictures do not rhyme.

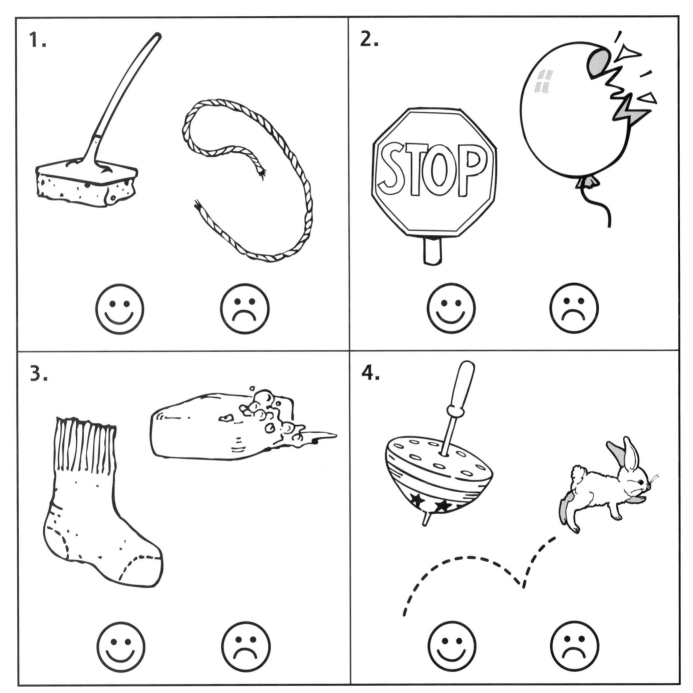

To the Teacher: Review the picture names with students.
(**1.** mop, rope; **2.** stop, pop; **3.** sock, soap; **4.** top, hop)

Finding rhyming pairs

Phonemic Awareness

The Top
and the Goat

Say the name of each picture.
Glue them in sets that rhyme.

glue	glue
glue	glue
glue	glue

Identifying words that rhyme

Phonemic Awareness   Basic Phonics Skills, Level A • EMC 3318 • ©2004 by Evan-Moor Corp.

Name —————————————————————

Color the picture if it rhymes with **bed**.

To the Teacher: Review the picture names with students.
(red, jet, thread, sled, pin, bread)

Identifying words that rhyme

Find the Rhyme

Circle the pictures in each row that rhyme.

1.

2.

3.

4.

To the Teacher: Review the picture names with students.
(**1.** red, jet, sled; **2.** mop, bed, hop; **3.** thread, rip, bread; **4.** goat, soap, rope)

Distinguishing rhyming words

The Jeep

Color the picture if it rhymes with **jeep**.

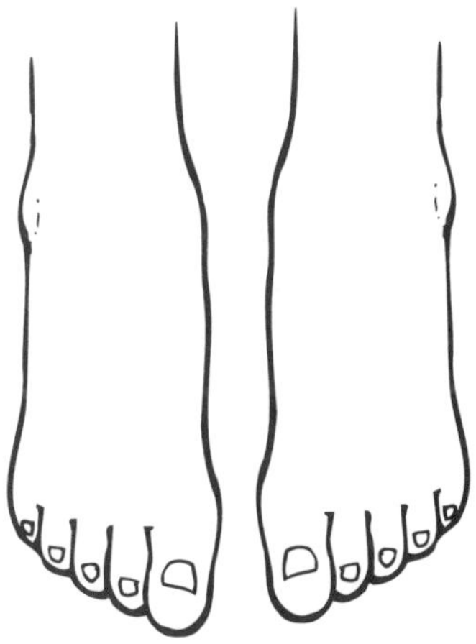

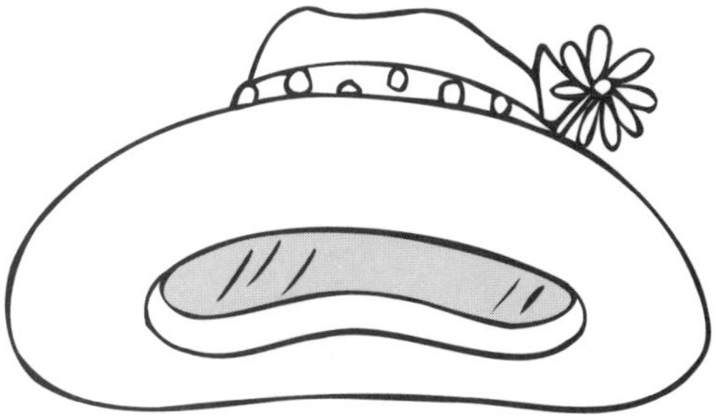

To the Teacher: Review the picture names with students.
(sheep, leaf, feet, sleep, sweep, hat)

Identifying words that rhyme

Phonemic Awareness

79

Name _____

Find the Rhyme

Circle the pictures in each row that rhyme.

1.

2.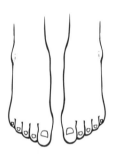

3.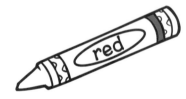

4.  10

To the Teacher: Review the picture names with students.
(**1.** sleep, leaf, sweep; **2.** feet, sheep, peep; **3.** red, beep, bed; **4.** mop, ten, top)

Distinguishing rhyming words

Basic Phonics Skills, Level A • EMC 3318 • ©2004 by Evan-Moor Corp.

Rhyming Pairs

Say the names of the pictures.

Circle 😊 if the pictures rhyme.

Circle 🙁 if the pictures do <u>not</u> rhyme.

To the Teacher: Review the picture names with students.
(**1.** jeep, sweep; **2.** feet, sheep; **3.** leaf, peep; **4.** beep, sleep)

Finding rhyming pairs

The Jeep and the Bed

Say the name of each picture.
Glue them in sets that rhyme.

glue	glue
glue	glue
glue	glue

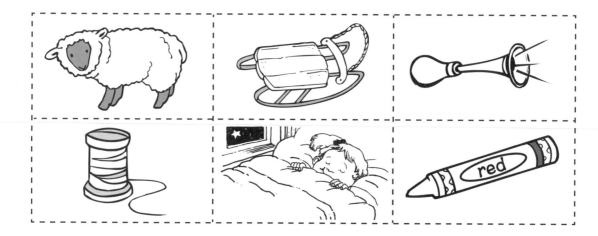

Identifying words that rhyme

Color the picture if it rhymes with **bug**.

Hug Bug

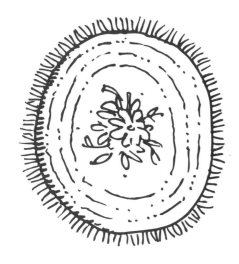

To the Teacher: Review the picture names with students.
(rug, top, hug, mug, jug, sun)

Identifying words that rhyme

Name

Circle the pictures in each row that rhyme.

1.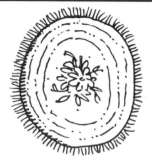

2.

3.

4.

To the Teacher: Review the picture names with students.
(**1.** rug, duck, bug; **2.** hug, jug, dog; **3.** mug, sun, plug; **4.** bug, log, mug)

Distinguishing rhyming words

Rhyming Pairs

Say the names of the pictures.

Circle 😊 if the pictures rhyme.

Circle ☹ if the pictures do **not** rhyme.

1.

2.

3.

4.

To the Teacher: Review the picture names with students.
(**1.** rug, mug; **2.** log, hug; **3.** sun, plug; **4.** bug, jug)

Finding rhyming pairs

Color the picture if it rhymes with **drum**.

The Drum

To the Teacher: Review the picture names with students.
(thumb, sun, gum, truck, ten, plum)

Identifying words that rhyme

Circle the pictures in each row that rhyme.

1.

2.  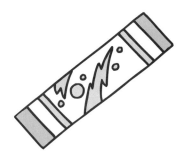 m m m m m m

3.

4.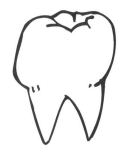

To the Teacher: Review the picture names with students.
(**1.** thumb, gum, sun; **2.** plum, dog, hum; **3.** sun, drum, plum; **4.** tooth, sheep, sweep)

Distinguishing rhyming words

Rhyming Pairs

Say the names of the pictures.

Circle 😊 if the pictures rhyme.

Circle ☹ if the pictures do <u>not</u> rhyme.

To the Teacher: Review the picture names with students.
(**1.** gum, plum; **2.** sun, thumb; **3.** drum, gum; **4.** truck, hum)

Finding rhyming pairs

Drum and Bug

Say the name of each picture.
Glue them in sets that rhyme.

glue	glue
glue	glue
glue	glue

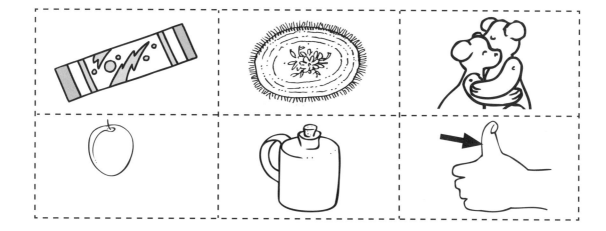

Identifying words that rhyme

Name -

Color the picture if it rhymes with **track**.

To the Teacher: Review the picture names with students.
(tack, sack, duck, backpack, black, jam)

Identifying words that rhyme

Find the Rhyme

Circle the pictures in each row that rhyme.

1.

2.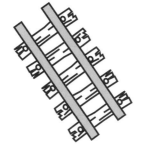

3.

4.

To the Teacher: Review the picture names with students.
(**1.** back, truck, stack; **2.** bat, track, crack; **3.** black, sack, pan; **4.** tacks, hat, tracks)

Distinguishing rhyming words

Rhyming Pairs

Say the names of the pictures.

Circle 😊 if the pictures rhyme.

Circle 😞 if the pictures do not rhyme.

To the Teacher: Review the picture names with students.
(**1.** hat, crack; **2.** track, pan; **3.** tack, black; **4.** stacks, tracks)

Finding rhyming pairs

Phonemic Awareness   Basic Phonics Skills, Level A • EMC 3318 • ©2004 by Evan-Moor Corp.

Name -

Color the picture if it rhymes with **chick**.

To the Teacher: Review the picture names with students.
(stick, duck, lick, kick, brick, pig)

Identifying words that rhyme

Name _____

Find the Rhyme

Circle the pictures in each row that rhyme.

1.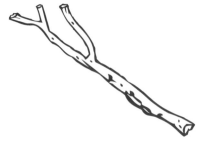

2.

3.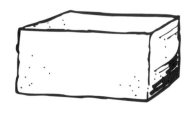

4.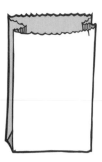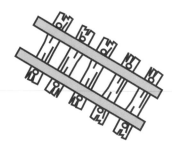

To the Teacher: Review the picture names with students.
(**1.** lick, ship, stick; **2.** clock, chick, pick; **3.** brick, kick, lock; **4.** bat, sack, track)

Distinguishing rhyming words

Phonemic Awareness Basic Phonics Skills, Level A • EMC 3318 • ©2004 by Evan-Moor Corp.

Name

Rhyming Pairs

Say the names of the pictures.

Circle 😊 if the pictures rhyme.

Circle 🙁 if the pictures do not rhyme.

To the Teacher: Review the picture names with students.
(**1.** kick, stick; **2.** lock, brick; **3.** trick, clock; **4.** pick, chick)

Finding rhyming pairs

Chick or Track?

Say the name of each picture.
Glue them in sets that rhyme.

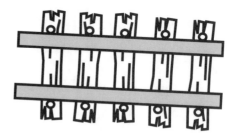

glue	glue
glue	glue
glue	glue

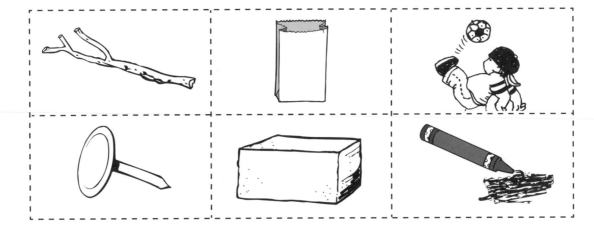

Distinguishing rhyming words

Basic Phonics Skills, Level A • EMC 3318 • ©2004 by Evan-Moor Corp.

Color the picture if it rhymes with **lock**.

Lock It!

To the Teacher: Review the picture names with students.
(clock, rock, sock, frog, block, duck)

Identifying words that rhyme

Circle the pictures in each row that rhyme.

Find the Rhyme

1.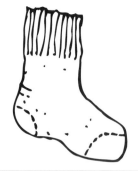

2.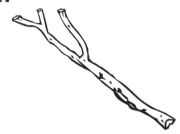

3.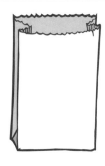

4.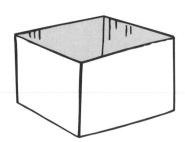

To the Teacher: Review the picture names with students.
(**1.** sock, truck, block; **2.** stick, lock, rock; **3.** clock, sock, sack; **4.** block, box, "tock")

Distinguishing rhyming words

Basic Phonics Skills, Level A • EMC 3318 • ©2004 by Evan-Moor Corp.

Name

Rhyming Pairs

Say the names of the pictures.

Circle 😊 if the pictures rhyme.

Circle ☹ if the pictures do not rhyme.

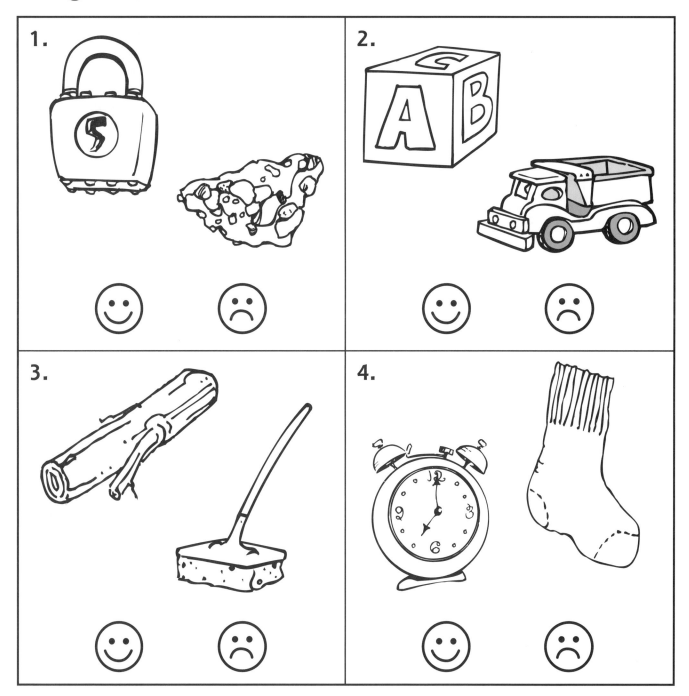

To the Teacher: Review the picture names with students.
(**1.** lock, rock; **2.** block, truck; **3.** log, mop; **4.** clock, sock)

Finding rhyming pairs

A Sock and a Brick

Say the name of each picture.
Glue them in sets that rhyme.

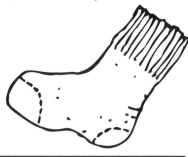

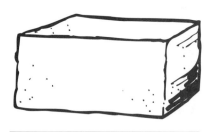

glue	glue
glue	glue
glue	glue

Distinguishing rhyming words

Name _____

Circle the pictures in each row that begin with the same sound as the first one.

To the Teacher: Review the picture names with students.
(**1.** cat, cake, top, car; **2.** mop, net, mouse, man; **3.** sun, soap, scissors, fish; **4.** bat, bed, duck, bike)

Identifying beginning sounds

Name _____

Circle the pictures in each row that begin with the same sound as the first one.

To the Teacher: Review the picture names with students.
(**1.** goat, kite, gum, gate; **2.** lamp, lemon, horse, lips; **3.** pig, paint, pen, boy; **4.** toe, ten, doll, tub)

Identifying beginning sounds

Beginning Sounds

Say the names of the pictures.

Circle 😊 if the pictures begin with the same sound.

Circle 🙁 if the pictures do not begin with the same sound.

To the Teacher: Review the picture names with students.
(**1.** duck, dog; **2.** hat, hug; **3.** bus, cat; **4.** rock, rug; **5.** pie, pig; **6.** mask, mouse)

Identifying beginning sounds

Match Them Up

Listen for the beginning sounds.
Draw lines to match.

1.  •   •

2.  •   •

3.  •   •

4.  •   •

5.  •   •

To the Teacher: Review the picture names with students.
(**1.** vest, **2.** nine, **3.** bird, **4.** goat, **5.** yarn; nest, barn, yo-yo, van, gopher)

Identifying beginning sounds

Name ---

Circle the pictures in each row that end with the same sound as the first one.

To the Teacher: Review the picture names with students.
(**1.** tub, crib, bib, pig; **2.** jet, cup, foot, boat; **3.** drum, jam, broom, sun; **4.** duck, brick, bat, hook)

Identifying ending sounds

Name _____

Circle the pictures in each row that end with
the same sound as the first one.

To the Teacher: Review the picture names with students.
(**1.** dog, pig, sad, bug; **2.** doll, hat, ball, girl; **3.** pen, fan, mop, sun; **4.** bus, kiss, gas, leaf)

Identifying ending sounds

Name _____

What Comes at the End?

Say the names of the pictures.

Circle ☺ if the pictures end with the same sound.

Circle ☹ if the pictures do <u>not</u> end with the same sound.

To the Teacher: Review the picture names with students.
(**1.** lip, pig; **2.** star, four; **3.** top, cup; **4.** sock, lock; **5.** coat, hat; **6.** hive, five)

Identifying ending sounds

Phonemic Awareness

Name ─────────────

Listen for the ending sounds.
Draw lines to match.

1.  •

                                                     •

2.  •

                                                     •

3.  •

                                                     •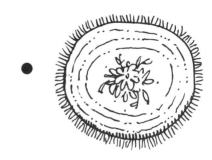

4.  •

                                                     •

5.  •

                                                     •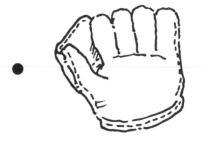

To the Teacher: Review the picture names with students.
(**1.** wig, **2.** ten, **3.** tub, **4.** gum, **5.** bat; jam, crab, rug, pan, mitt)

Identifying ending sounds

How Many Sounds?

Count the sounds in each word.
Fill in the circles to show how many you hear.

1.

LUIGI'S
Spaghetti
Curlys

● ● ● ○

2.

○ ○ ○ ○

3.

○ ○ ○ ○

4.

○ ○ ○ ○

5.

○ ○ ○ ○

6.

10

○ ○ ○ ○

To the Teacher: Review the picture names with students. Have students say the word, separate and count the sounds, then repeat the word again.
(**1.** can, **2.** pie, **3.** nest, **4.** top, **5.** bats, **6.** ten)

Practice counting sounds (phonemes)

Listen and Count

Count the sounds in each word.
Fill in the circles to show how many you hear.

1.

○ ○ ○ ○

2.

○ ○ ○ ○

3.

○ ○ ○ ○

4.

○ ○ ○ ○

5.

○ ○ ○ ○

6.

○ ○ ○ ○

To the Teacher: Review the picture names with students. Have students say the word, separate and count the sounds, then say the word again. (**1.** boat, **2.** bow, **3.** bus, **4.** key, **5.** sun, **6.** jeep)

Practice counting sounds (phonemes)

Name _____

Two, Three, Four!

Count the sounds in each word.
Circle the number to show how many you hear.

1.

2   3   4

2.

2   3   4

3.

2   3   4

4.

2   3   4

5.

2   3   4

6.

2   3   4

To the Teacher: Review the picture names with students. Have students say the word, separate and count the sounds, then say the word again. (**1.** dog, **2.** van, **3.** sock, **4.** bee, **5.** tent, **6.** knife)

Practice counting sounds (phonemes)

Phonemic Awareness

Name

Count the Sounds

Count the sounds in each word.
Circle the number to show how many you hear.

1.

2   3   4

2.

2   3   4

3.

2   3   4

4.

2   3   4

5.

2   3   4

6.

2   3   4

To the Teacher: Review the picture names with students. Have students say the word, separate and count the sounds, then say the word again. (**1.** egg, **2.** cake, **3.** coats, **4.** hand, **5.** pot, **6.** ball)

Practice counting sounds (phonemes)

Alphabetic Awareness

Identifying and writing uppercase and lowercase letters.

BASIC Phonics Skills

Traditional Manuscript Alphabet

Basic Phonics Skills, Level A • EMC 3318 • ©2004 by Evan-Moor Corp.

Name _____

A a
apple

Trace and write the letters.

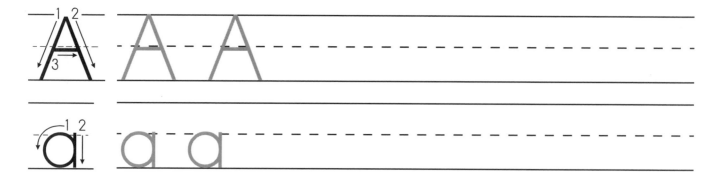

Circle Ⓐ. Box a.

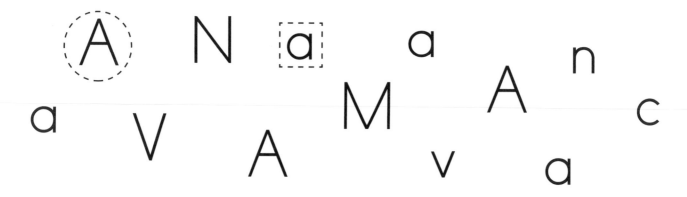

Name -

apple

Trace and write the letters.

A A A

a a a

Circle Ⓐ. Box [a].

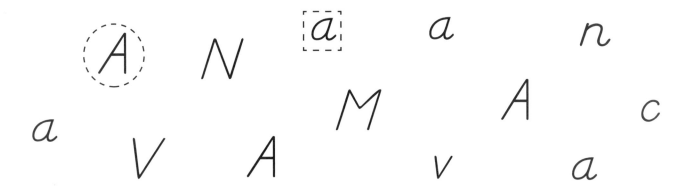

Name

B b
bat

Trace and write the letters.

B B B

b b b

Circle the one that matches the first one.

B	A	E	B	R
b	r	a	b	d

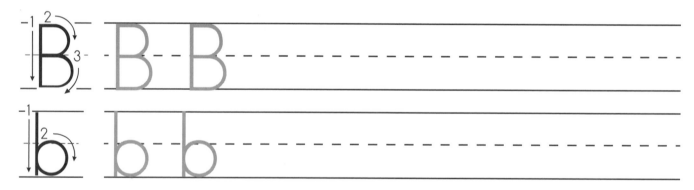

Identifying and writing uppercase and lowercase B, b

Basic Phonics Skills, Level A • EMC 3318 • ©2004 by Evan-Moor Corp.

Name _____

B b
bat

Trace and write the letters.

B B

b b

Circle the one that matches the first one.

B	A	E	B	R
b	r	a	b	d

Identifying and writing uppercase and lowercase B, b

Name _____

C c
cake

Trace and write the letters.

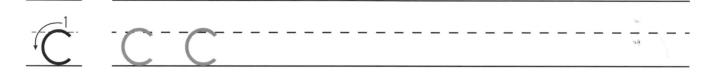

Draw lines to match.

A   c

B   a

C   b

Identifying and writing uppercase and lowercase C, c

Basic Phonics Skills, Level A • EMC 3318 • ©2004 by Evan-Moor Corp.

Cc
cake

Trace and write the letters.

C C C C

c c c

Draw lines to match.

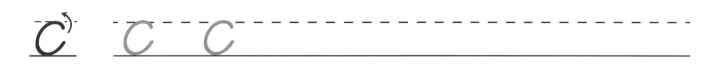

A c

B a

C b

Identifying and writing uppercase and lowercase C, c

Name _____

Dd
duck

Trace and write the letters.

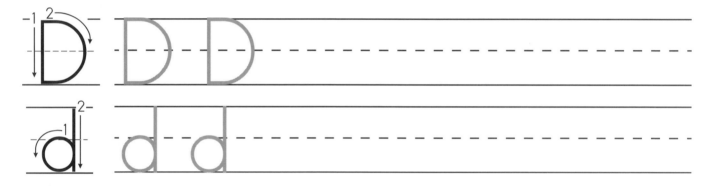

Circle D. Box d.

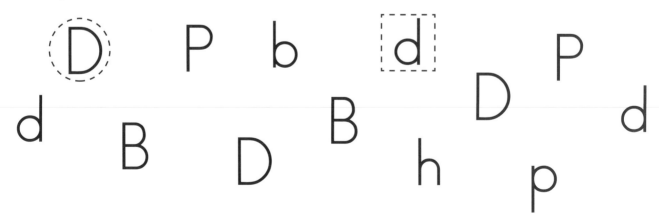

Identifying and writing uppercase and lowercase D, d

Basic Phonics Skills, Level A • EMC 3318 • ©2004 by Evan-Moor Corp.

Name _____

Dd
duck

Trace and write the letters.

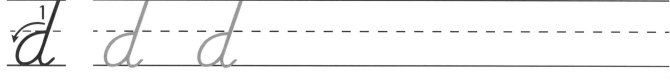

Circle ⓓ. Box 🄳.

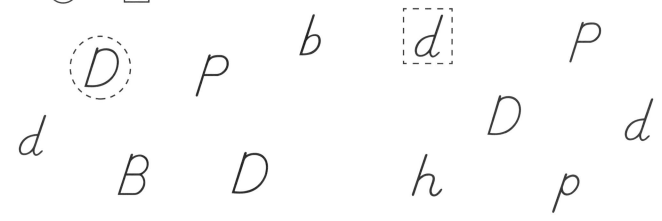

Identifying and writing uppercase and lowercase D, d

Alphabetic Awareness 123

Name

 Ee
egg

Trace and write the letters.

 E E

 e e

Circle the one that matches the first one.

E	F	E	B	H
e	c	a	e	o

Identifying and writing uppercase and lowercase E, e

124 **Alphabetic Awareness**   Basic Phonics Skills, Level A • EMC 3318 • ©2004 by Evan-Moor Corp.

Name --------------------------------

Ee
egg

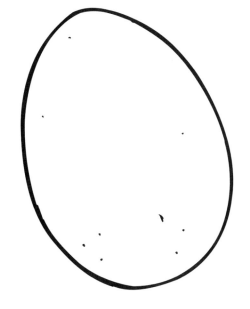

Trace and write the letters.

1 2→
3→
4→

E   E   E

e   e   e

Circle the one that matches the first one.

E	F	E	B	H
e	c	a	e	o

Identifying and writing uppercase and lowercase E, e

Name _____

Ff

fish

Trace and write the letters.

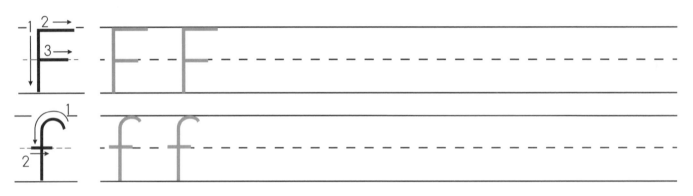

Draw lines to match.

F   d

B   f

D   b

Identifying and writing uppercase and lowercase F, f

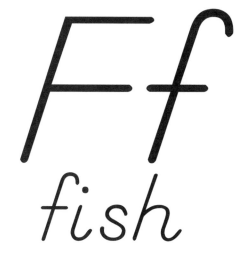

fish

Trace and write the letters.

$\underset{\downarrow}{\overset{1\ 2\rightarrow}{\cancel{F}}}$ F F - - - - - - - - - - - - - - -

$\underset{2\rightarrow}{\overset{1}{f}}$ f f - - - - - - - - - - - - - - -

Draw lines to match.

F	d
B	f
D	b

Identifying and writing uppercase and lowercase F, f

Big G, Little g

Gg
goat

Trace and write the letters.

G G G

g g g

a   b   c   d   e   f

A   B   C

D   E   F

Identifying and writing uppercase and lowercase G, g

Basic Phonics Skills, Level A • EMC 3318 • ©2004 by Evan-Moor Corp.

G g
goat

Trace and write the letters.

G G G

g g g

a b c d e f

A B C

D E F

Identifying and writing uppercase and lowercase G, g

Name —

Hh
hen

Trace and write the letters.

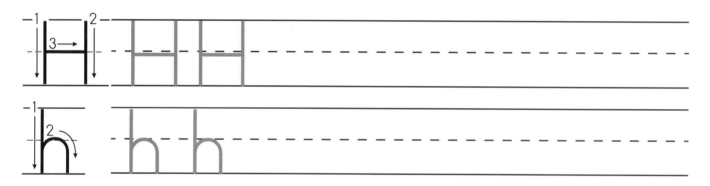

Circle (H). Box [h].

H   F   f   [h]   B

h   B   B   H

    b   b   f   b

Identifying and writing uppercase and lowercase H, h

Name

Big H, Little h

H h
hen

Trace and write the letters.

H H H

h h h

Circle (H) . Box [h] .

H   F   f   [h]   B

h   B   H   h

   B   b   B   f   b

Identifying and writing uppercase and lowercase H, h

Alphabetic Awareness

Name -

I i
igloo

Trace and write the letters.

2 →
1
↓
3 →

I I

1 •
↓

i i

Circle the one that matches the first one.

I	H	I	F	L
i	l	f	i	t

Identifying and writing uppercase and lowercase I, i

I i
igloo

Trace and write the letters.

2→
1 I   I   I

i   i   i
3→

Circle the one that matches the first one.

I	H	I	F	L
i	l	f	i	t

Identifying and writing uppercase and lowercase I, i

Name

Big J, Little j

J j

jeep

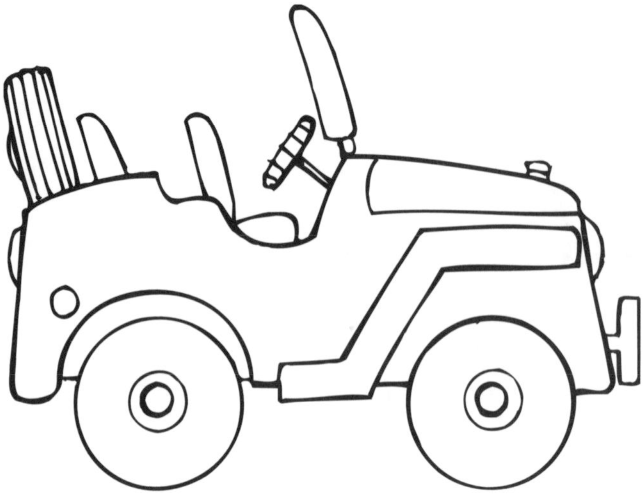

Trace and write the letters.

J J J

j j j

Draw lines to match.

J	g
G	d
D	j

Identifying and writing uppercase and lowercase J, j

Name

J j
jeep

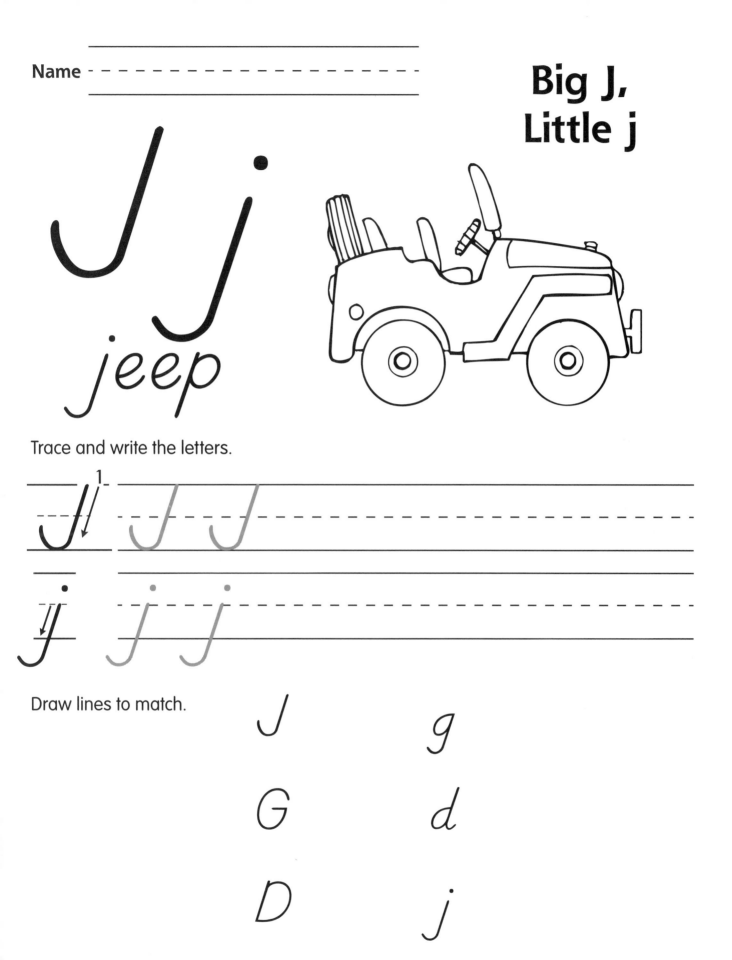

Trace and write the letters.

J¹ J J

j j j

Draw lines to match.

J   g

G   d

D   j

Identifying and writing uppercase and lowercase J, j

K k
koala

Trace and write the letters.

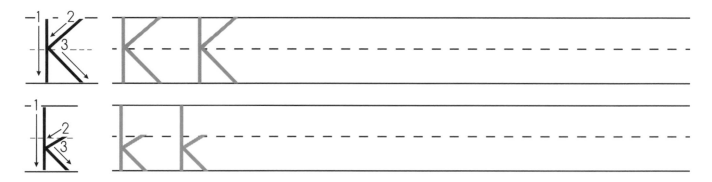

Circle Ⓚ. Box k.

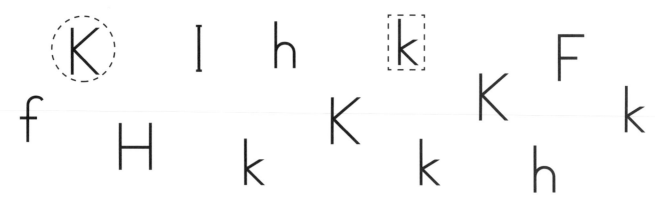

K k
koala

Trace and write the letters.

K   K   K

k   k   k

Circle (K). Box [k].

(K)   I   h   [k]   F

f   H   k   K   K   k

H   k   k   h

Identifying and writing uppercase and lowercase K, k

Name _____

L l
leaf

Trace and write the letters.

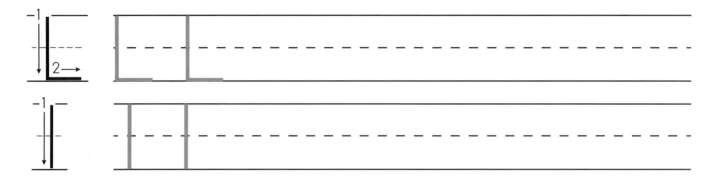

Circle the one that matches the first one.

L	l	F	L	H
l	i	f	l	h

Identifying and writing uppercase and lowercase L, l

Basic Phonics Skills, Level A • EMC 3318 • ©2004 by Evan-Moor Corp.

Name

L l
leaf

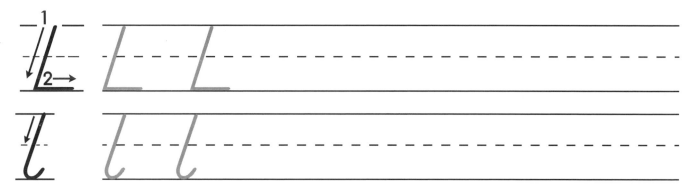

Trace and write the letters.

Circle the one that matches the first one.

L	I	F	L	H
l	i	f	l	h

Identifying and writing uppercase and lowercase L, l

Name _____

Mm
moon

Trace and write the letters.

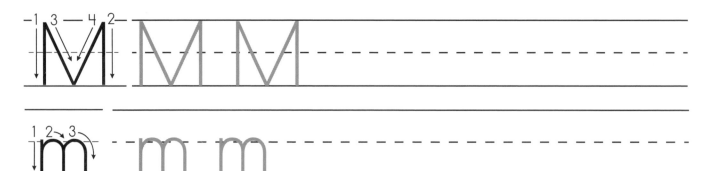

M M M

m m m

h	i	j	k	l	m

H   I   J

K   L   M

Identifying and writing uppercase and lowercase M, m

Name _____

Mm
moon

1 3 4 2
M M M
m m m

h   i   j   k   l   m

H   I   J
K   L   M

Identifying and writing uppercase and lowercase M, m

Name _____

N n

nest

Trace and write the letters.

N

n

Circle the one that matches the first one.

N	M	N	H	V
n	r	h	n	m

Identifying and writing uppercase and lowercase N, n

Name _____

N n
nest

Trace and write the letters.

N   N N

n   n n

Circle the one that matches the first one.

N	M	N	H	V
n	r	h	n	m

Identifying and writing uppercase and lowercase N, n

Name _____

OX

Trace and write the letters.

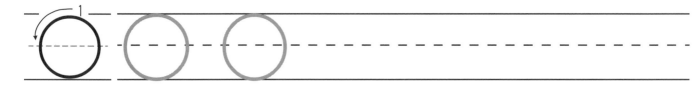

Circle ⬭. Box ◻.

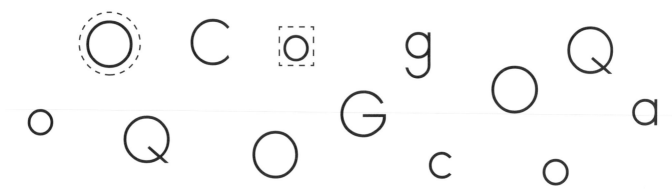

Identifying and writing uppercase and lowercase O, o

Name _____

Big O,
Little o

OX

Trace and write the letters.

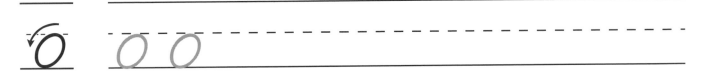

Circle ⃝O. Box ▢o.

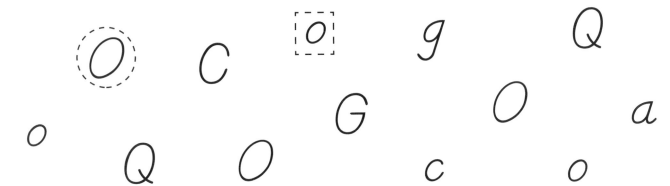

Identifying and writing uppercase and lowercase O, o

Alphabetic Awareness

P p
pig

Trace and write the letters.

P   P P -

p   p p -

Draw lines to match.

P	d
B	p
D	b

Identifying and writing uppercase and lowercase P, p

P p

pig

Trace and write the letters.

P P P P

p p p p

Draw lines to match.

P   d

B   p

D   b

Identifying and writing uppercase and lowercase P, p

Name _____

 queen

Trace and write the letters.

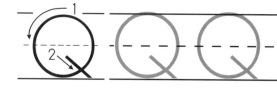

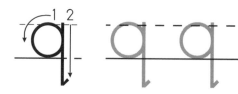

Circle Ⓠ. Box q̄.

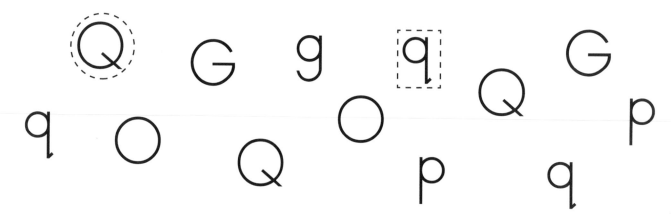

Identifying and writing uppercase and lowercase Q, q

Basic Phonics Skills, Level A • EMC 3318 • ©2004 by Evan-Moor Corp.

Name _____

Qq
queen

Trace and write the letters.

  $Q \quad Q$

  $q \quad q$

Circle . Box .

 G g G

q O Q O Q p

p q

Identifying and writing uppercase and lowercase Q, q

Name _____

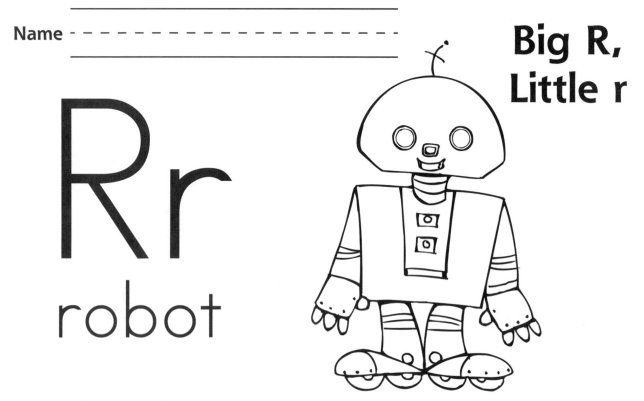

Rr
robot

Trace and write the letters.

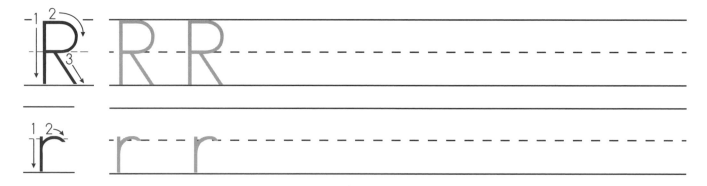

Circle the one that matches the first one.

R	B	R	P	F
r	n	h	r	c

Identifying and writing uppercase and lowercase R, r

Name

R r
robot

Trace and write the letters.

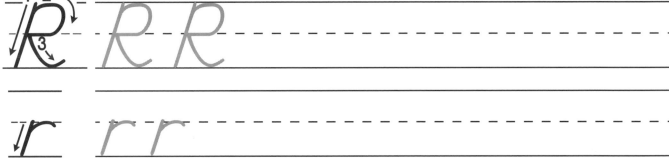

Circle the one that matches the first one.

R	B	R	P	F
r	n	h	r	c

Identifying and writing uppercase and lowercase R, r

Name

S s
sun

Trace and write the letters.

S S S

s s s

Write the correct one on the line.

| n | o | p | q | r | s |

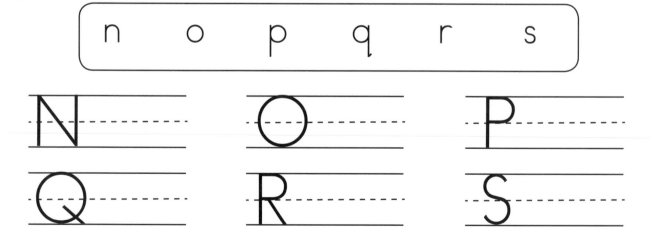

N   O   P

Q   R   S

Identifying and writing uppercase and lowercase S, s

Name _____

S s
sun

Trace and write the letters.

S S S

s s s

Write the correct one on the line.

n	o	p	q	r	s

N   O   P

Q   R   S

Identifying and writing uppercase and lowercase S, s

Name _____

T t

tent

Trace and write the letters.

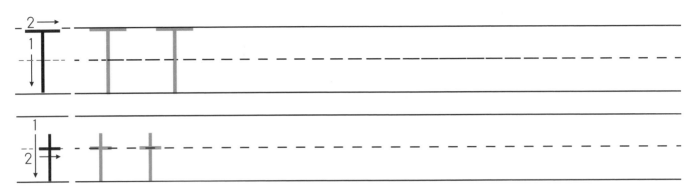

Draw lines to match.

T   f

I   t

F   i

Identifying and writing uppercase and lowercase T, t

Name _____

Tt
tent

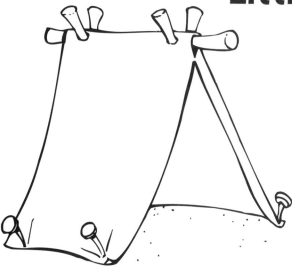

Trace and write the letters.

T T T

t t t

Draw lines to match.

T   f

I   t

F   i

Identifying and writing uppercase and lowercase T, t

Big U, Little u

U u

up

Trace and write the letters.

U U U

u u u

Circle the one that matches the first one.

U	J	U	Q	O
u	c	o	u	a

Identifying and writing uppercase and lowercase U, u

**Big U,
Little u**

U u

up

Trace and write the letters.

U U U

u u u

Circle the one that matches the first one.

U	J	U	Q	O
u	c	o	u	a

Identifying and writing uppercase and lowercase U, u

Name

Vv
van

Trace and write the letters.

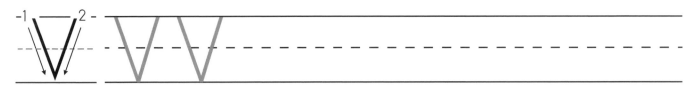

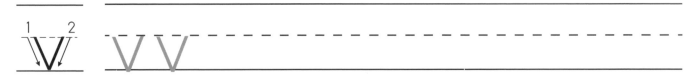

Circle ⓥ. Box v.

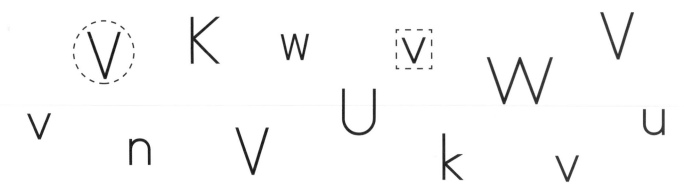

Identifying and writing uppercase and lowercase V, v

Basic Phonics Skills, Level A • EMC 3318 • ©2004 by Evan-Moor Corp.

van

Trace and write the letters.

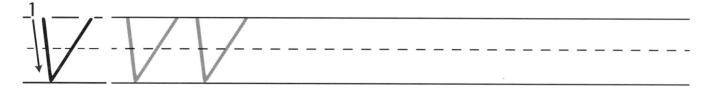

Circle (V). Box [v].

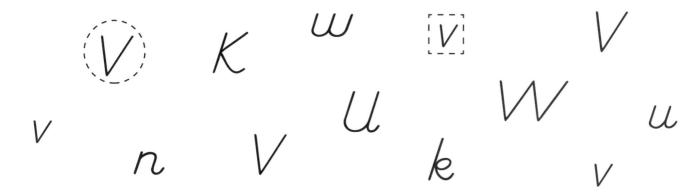

Identifying and writing uppercase and lowercase V, v

wagon

Trace and write the letters.

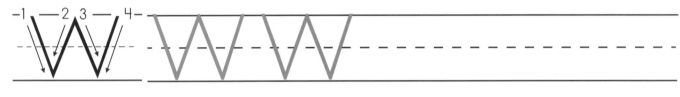

Draw lines to match.

W   u

V   w

U   v

Identifying and writing uppercase and lowercase W, w

Name ----------------------------------

Ww

wagon

Trace and write the letters.

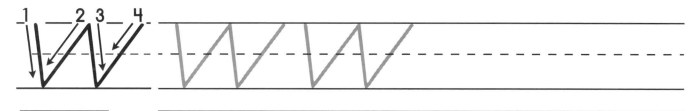

Draw lines to match.

Identifying and writing uppercase and lowercase W, w

Name _____

X x

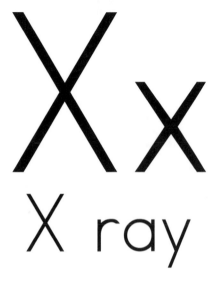

X ray

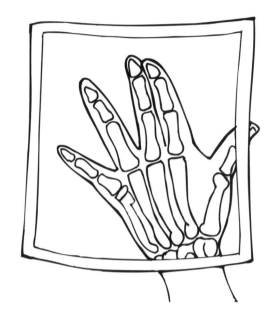

Trace and write the letters.

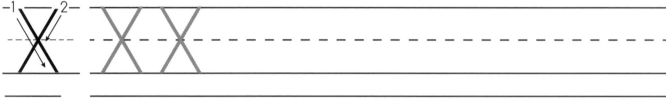

Write the correct one on the line.

| t | u | v | w | x | y |

T   U   V

W   X   Y

Identifying and writing uppercase and lowercase X, x

Name _____

X x

X ray

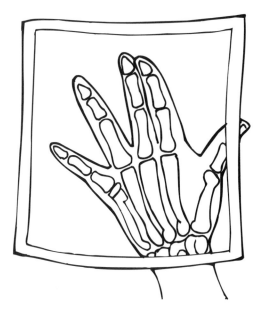

Trace and write the letters.

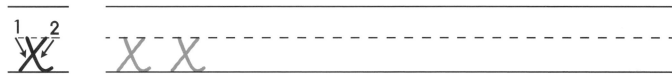

Write the correct one on the line.

| t | u | v | w | x | y |

T   U   V

W   X   Y

Identifying and writing uppercase and lowercase X, x

Name

Big Y, Little y

Yy

yo-yo

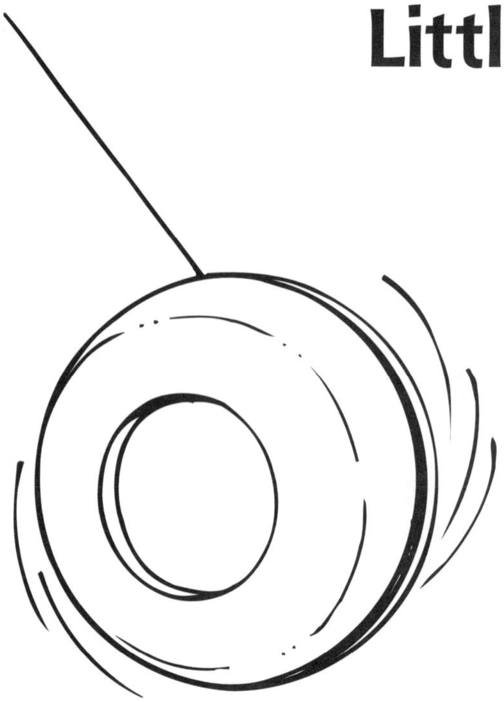

Trace and write the letters.

Y Y Y

y y y

Circle the one that matches the first one.

Y	V	Y	W	X
y	v	x	y	q

Identifying and writing uppercase and lowercase Y, y

Big Y, Little y

Yy
yo-yo

Trace and write the letters.

Y Y Y

y y y

Circle the one that matches the first one.

Y	V	Y	W	X
y	v	x	y	q

Identifying and writing uppercase and lowercase Y, y

Name _____

Z z
zebra

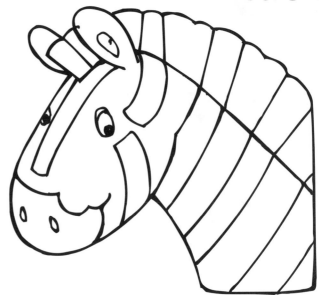

Trace and write the letters.

Z Z Z Z

Z Z Z

Circle Ⓩ. Box z .

Identifying and writing uppercase and lowercase Z, z

Basic Phonics Skills, Level A • EMC 3318 • ©2004 by Evan-Moor Corp.

Name

Z z
zebra

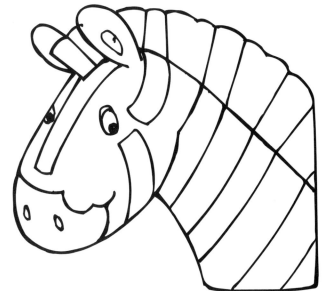

Trace and write the letters.

1 → Z Z Z

Z Z Z

Circle Ⓩ. Box [z].

Z W z w N

z   N Z v

V v v z

The Alphabet Capitals

Fill in the missing letters.

A   C   E

F   J

      N   P

     R   U

V   Y

Alphabet review

Name -

The Alphabet
Capitals

Fill in the missing letters.

A ___ C ___ E

E ___ ___ J

___ ___ N ___ P

___ R ___ ___ U

V ___ ___ Y

Alphabet review

©2004 by Evan-Moor Corp. • Basic Phonics Skills, Level A • EMC 3318   **Alphabetic Awareness**   **169**

Name

Fill in the missing letters.

The Alphabet
Lowercase

a ____ c ____ e

f ____ ____ j ____

____ ____ n ____ p

____ r ____ ____ u

v ____ ____ y ____

Alphabet review

a ___ *c* ___ *e*

f ___ ___ *j*

___ *n* ___ *p*

___ *r* ___ *u*

v ___ ___ *y*

Name _____

Copy the word.

 cat

_____

 hat

_____

 dog

_____

 fan

_____

Fill in the missing letter.

A B _____   k l _____

E F _____   n o _____

S T _____   d e _____

Alphabet review and handwriting practice

Sound-Symbol Association
A–Z

Aa
apple

Color the ones that begin like **apple**.

To the Teacher: Review the picture names with students.
(ant, cat, anchor, ax, antlers, ball)

Listening for initial short a

Name _____

Glue the pictures that begin with a **short a** under the apple.
Glue the other pictures under 🙁.

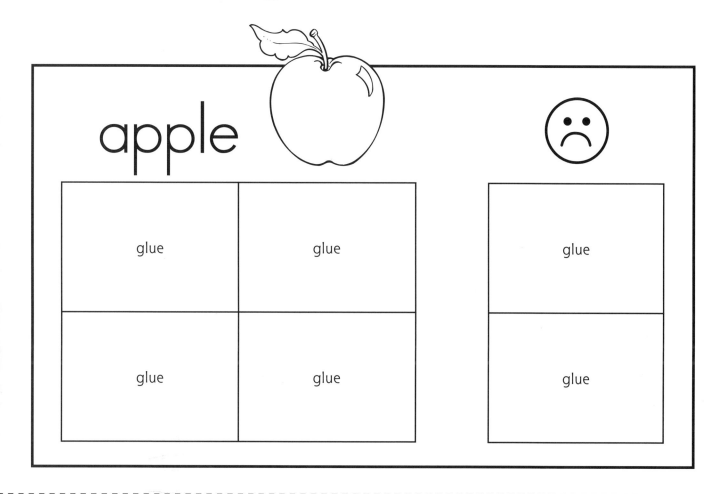

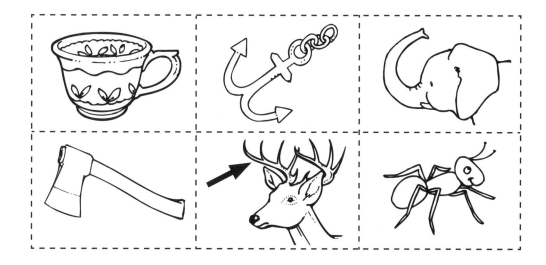

Listening for initial short a

Name _____

Color the things that begin like **apple**.

How many did you find? _____

To the Teacher: Review the picture names with students.
(apples, ant, antlers, chair, moose, book, glasses)
Listening for initial short a

Aa
apple

Listen for the Sound

B b
bat

Color the ones that begin like **bat**.

To the Teacher: Review the picture names with students.
(balloon, butterfly, dog, bus, ball, van)

Listening for initial b

Name _____

Cut and Sort

Glue the pictures that begin with **b** under the bat.
Glue the other pictures under 😞 .

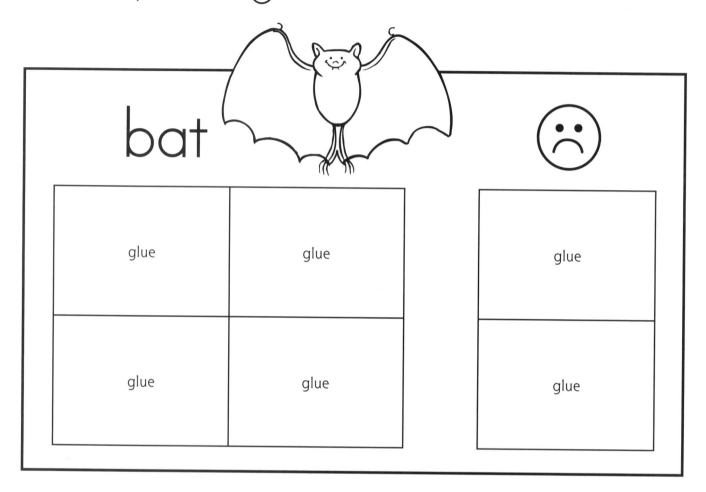

Listening for initial b

Basic Phonics Skills, Level A • EMC 3318 • ©2004 by Evan-Moor Corp.

Name _____

Color the things that begin like **bat**.

Bb
bat

How many did you find? _____

To the Teacher: Review the picture names with students.
(bear, balloon, ball, butterfly, shelf, bow tie)

Listening for initial b

Sound-Symbol Association **179**

Listen for the Sound

C c
cake

Color the ones that begin like **cake**.

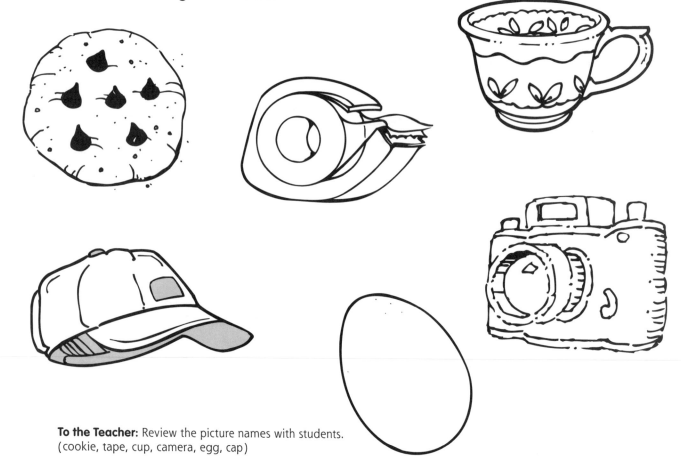

To the Teacher: Review the picture names with students.
(cookie, tape, cup, camera, egg, cap)

Listening for initial c

Name _____

Cut and Sort

Glue the pictures that begin with **c** under the cake.
Glue the other pictures under 😕.

cake

😕

glue	glue
glue	glue

glue
glue

Listening for initial c

Name

Color the things that begin like **cake**.

How many did you find? _____

To the Teacher: Review the picture names with students.
(cat, candle, cane, mouse, cheese, clock)

Listening for initial c

Cc
cake

Name

Dd
duck

Color the ones that begin like **duck**.

To the Teacher: Review the picture names with students.
(doll, dime, bear, door, vase, dog)

Listening for initial d

Name

Cut and Sort

Glue the pictures that begin with **d** under the duck.
Glue the other pictures under ☹.

duck

glue	glue
glue	glue

glue
glue

Listening for initial d

Sound-Symbol Association   Basic Phonics Skills, Level A • EMC 3318 • ©2004 by Evan-Moor Corp.

Name

What Do You See?

Color the things that begin like **duck**.

Dd
duck

How many did you find? _____

To the Teacher: Review the picture names with students.
(dog, daffodil, door, clock, table)

Listening for initial d

Sound-Symbol Association 185

Name _____

Ee
egg

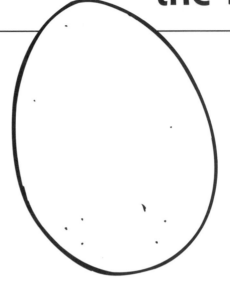

Color the ones that begin like **egg**.

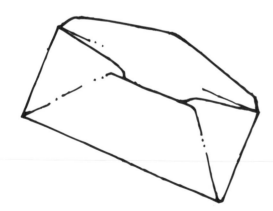

To the Teacher: Review the picture names with students. (shoe, apple, elf, hen, eskimo, envelope)

Listening for initial short e

Name _____

Glue the pictures that begin with a **short e** under the egg.
Glue the other pictures under 🙁.

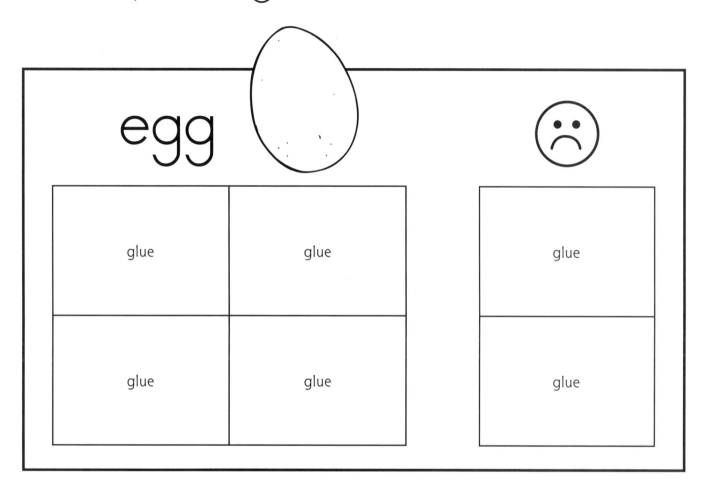

egg

glue	glue
glue	glue

🙁

glue
glue

Listening for initial short e

Name _____

What Do You See?

Color the things that begin like **egg**.

E e
egg

How many did you find? _____

To the Teacher: Review the picture names with students.
(elephant, envelope, Eskimo, pouch, hat)

Listening for initial short e

Name

F f

fish

Color the ones that begin like **fish**.

To the Teacher: Review the picture names with students.
(four, feather, sheep, fence, fan, van)

Listening for initial f

Name _____

Glue the pictures that begin with **f** under the fish.
Glue the other pictures under 😦 .

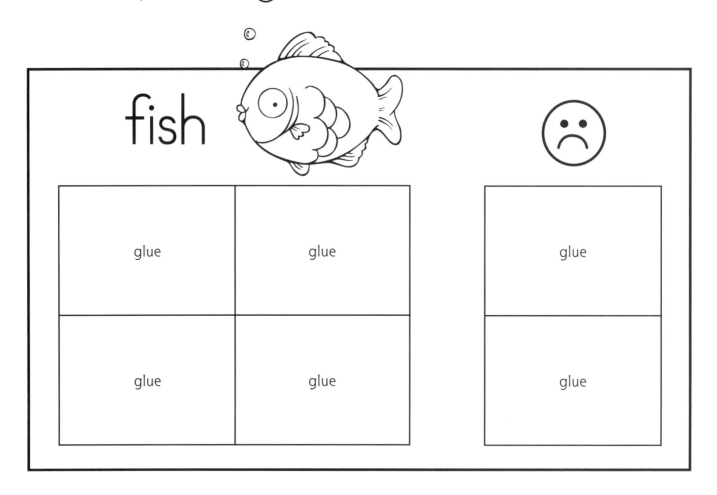

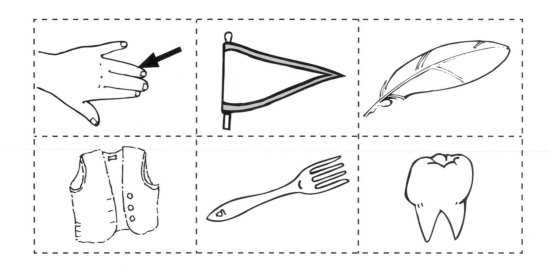

Listening for initial f

Name _____

What Do You See?

Color the things that begin like **fish**.

Ff
fish

How many did you find? _____

To the Teacher: Review the picture names with students.
(fox, flower, fence, bird, trees, feather)

Listening for initial f

Sound-Symbol Association

Name _____

Gg
goat

Color the ones that begin like **goat**.

To the Teacher: Review the picture names with students. (gate, eagle, gift, guitar, garbage can, coat)

Listening for initial g

Name _____

Glue the pictures that begin with **g** under the goat.
Glue the other pictures under .

goat

glue	glue
glue	glue

glue
glue

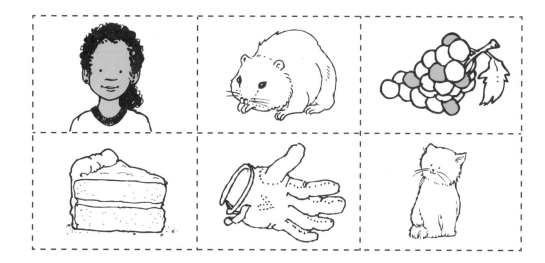

What Do You See?

Color the things that begin like **goat**.

How many did you find? _____

To the Teacher: Review the picture names with students.
(gorilla, guitar, goose, grass, sun, clouds)

Listening for initial g

Gg
goat

Basic Phonics Skills, Level A • EMC 3318 • ©2004 by Evan-Moor Corp.

Name _____

Hh
hen

Color the ones that begin like **hen**.

To the Teacher: Review the picture names with students.
(kite, nest, house, hose, hand, heart)

Listening for initial h

Sound-Symbol Association

Cut and Sort

Glue the pictures that begin with **h** under the hen.
Glue the other pictures under 😞 .

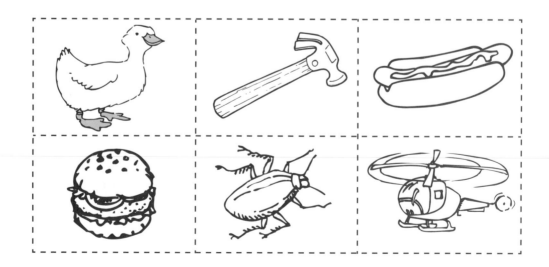

Listening for initial h

Basic Phonics Skills, Level A • EMC 3318 • ©2004 by Evan-Moor Corp.

Name _____

Color the things that begin like **hen**.

What Do You See?

How many did you find? _____

To the Teacher: Review the picture names with students.
(horse, hat, hose, hearts, sun, clouds, flower)

Hh
hen

Listening for initial h

©2004 by Evan-Moor Corp. • Basic Phonics Skills, Level A • EMC 3318

Sound-Symbol Association 197

Listen for the Sound

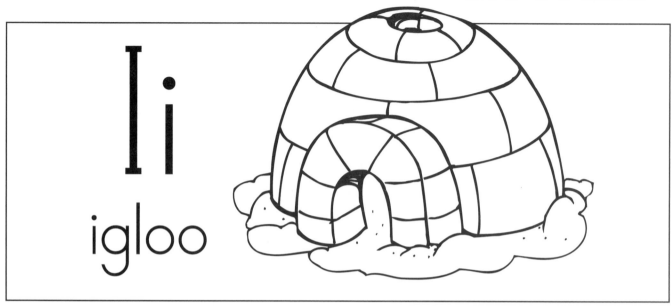

I i

igloo

Color the ones that begin like **igloo**.

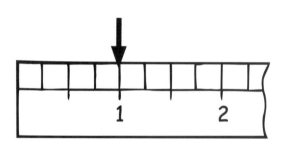

1   2

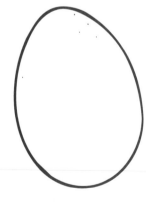

To the Teacher: Review the picture names with students.
(inch, insects, egg, instruments, pig)

Listening for initial short i

Name _____

Glue the pictures that begin with a **short i** under the igloo.
Glue the other pictures under 🙁.

igloo

glue	glue
glue	glue

glue
glue

Listening for initial short i

What Do You See?

Color the things that begin like **igloo**.

I i
igloo

How many did you find? _____

To the Teacher: Review the picture names with students.
(man, insects, ink, paper, quill pen, inchworm)
Listening for initial short i

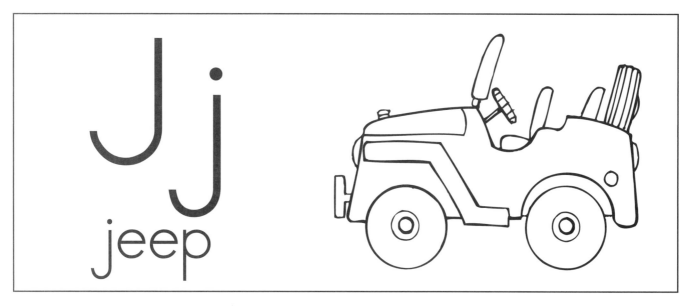

Color the ones that begin like **jeep**.

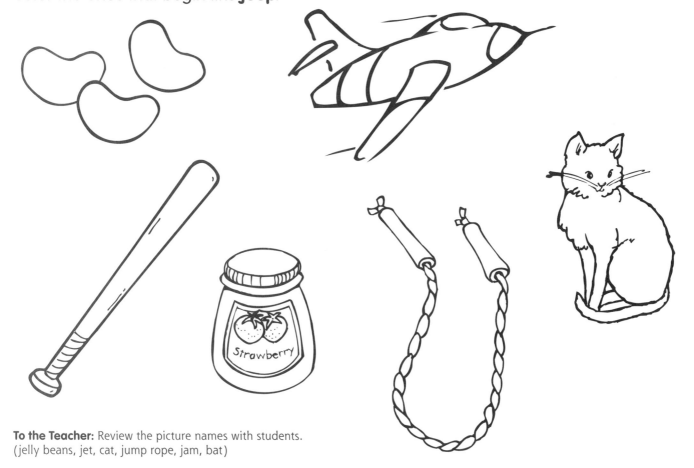

To the Teacher: Review the picture names with students.
(jelly beans, jet, cat, jump rope, jam, bat)

Cut and Sort

Glue the pictures that begin with **j** under the jeep.
Glue the other pictures under ☹.

jeep

☹

glue	glue		glue
glue	glue		glue

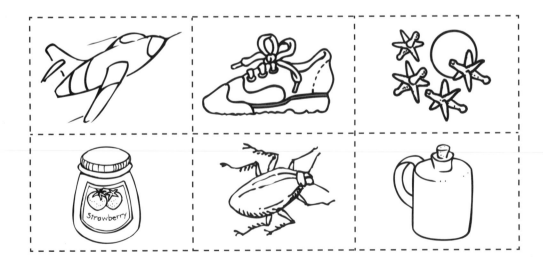

Listening for initial j

Name _____

Color the things that begin like **jeep**.

Jj
jeep

How many did you find? _____

To the Teacher: Review the picture names with students.
(jack-in-the-box, jelly beans, jump rope, jar)

Listening for initial j

Name ‒ ‒ ‒ ‒ ‒ ‒ ‒ ‒ ‒ ‒ ‒ ‒ ‒ ‒ ‒ ‒

Listen for the Sound

Kk
koala

Color the ones that begin like **koala**.

To the Teacher: Review the picture names with students.
(kangaroo, kite, top, key, king, dog)

Listening for initial k

Sound-Symbol Association Basic Phonics Skills, Level A • EMC 3318 • ©2004 by Evan-Moor Corp.

Name _____

Glue the pictures that begin with **k** under the koala.
Glue the other pictures under 😦.

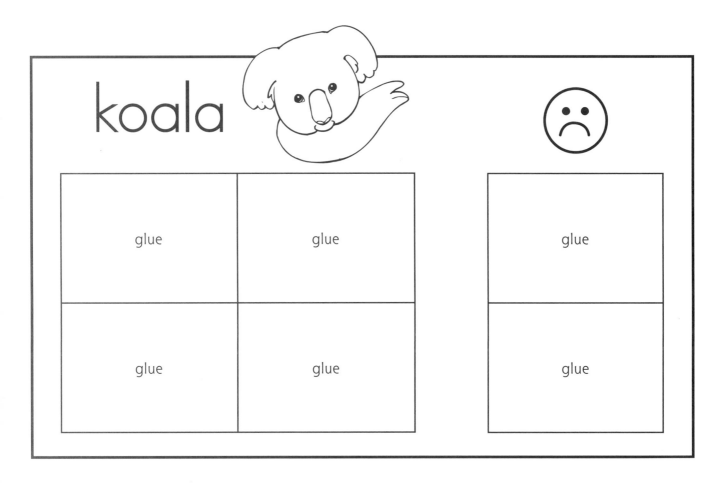

koala

😦

glue	glue
glue	glue

glue
glue

Listening for initial k

What Do You See?

Color the things that begin like **koala**.

How many did you find? _____

To the Teacher: Review the picture names with students.
(king, kangaroo, kite, kiwi, string, sun)
Listening for initial k

Kk
koala

Ll
leaf

Color the ones that begin like **leaf**.

To the Teacher: Review the picture names with students.
(log, lemons, rabbit, ladder, lion, ball)

Listening for initial l

Cut and Sort

Glue the pictures that begin with **l** under the leaf.
Glue the other pictures under ☹.

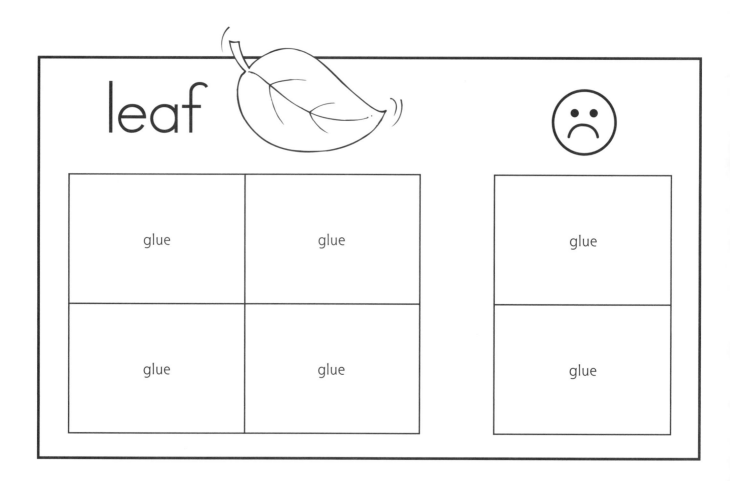

leaf ☹

glue	glue
glue	glue

glue
glue

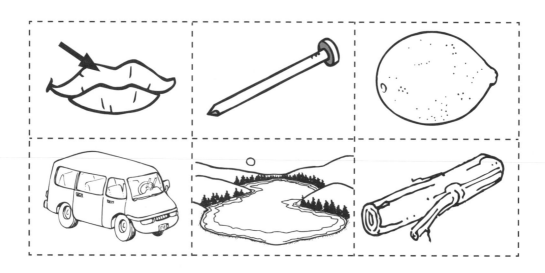

Listening for initial l

Name - - - - - - - - - - - - - - - - -

Color the things that begin like **leaf**.

How many did you find? _____

To the Teacher: Review the picture names with students.
(lion, lamb, ladybug, ladder, tree, grass)

Ll
leaf

Listening for initial l

Name _____

Mm
moon

Color the ones that begin like **moon**.

To the Teacher: Review the picture names with students.
(mitt, monkey, nickel, mop, lemon, mouse)

Listening for initial m

Basic Phonics Skills, Level A • EMC 3318 • ©2004 by Evan-Moor Corp.

Name _____

Glue the pictures that begin with **m** under the moon.
Glue the other pictures under 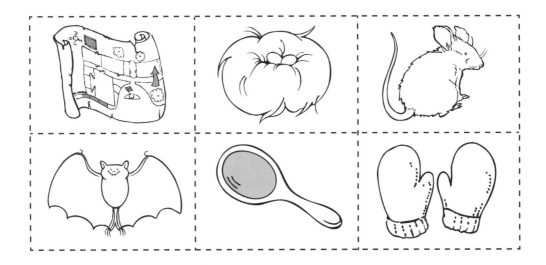.

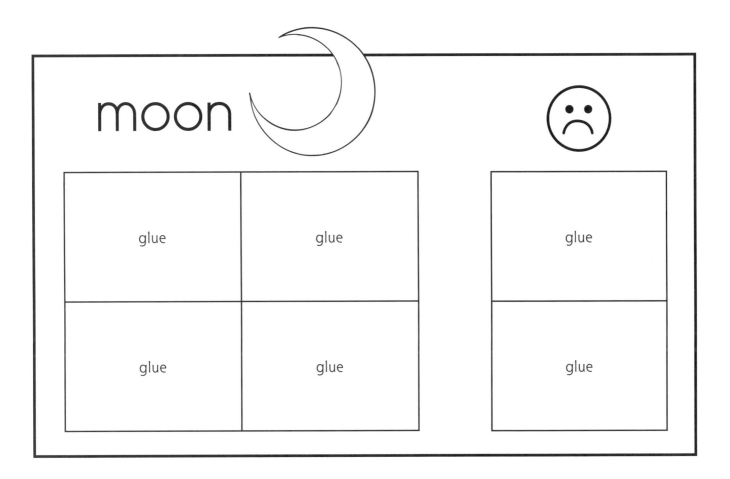

Name

Color the things that begin like **moon**.

How many did you find? _____

Mm
moon

To the Teacher: Review the picture names with students.
(monkey, mop, mouse, pail, puddle)
Listening for initial m

Basic Phonics Skills, Level A • EMC 3318 • ©2004 by Evan-Moor Corp.

Listen for the Sound

N n
nest

Color the ones that begin like **nest**.

To the Teacher: Review the picture names with students.
(nut, lock, necklace, mitten, nickel, net)

Listening for initial n

Name

Cut and Sort

Glue the pictures that begin with **n** under the nest.
Glue the other pictures under 😞 .

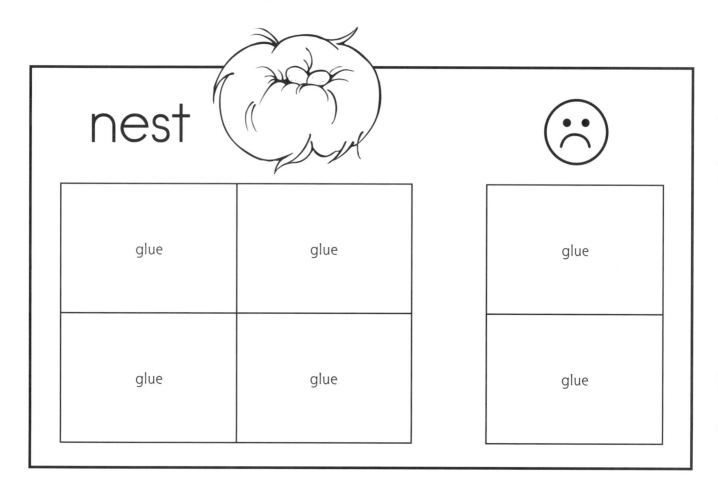

nest

glue	glue
glue	glue

😞
glue
glue

Listening for initial n

Basic Phonics Skills, Level A • EMC 3318 • ©2004 by Evan-Moor Corp.

Name _____

Color the things that begin like **nest**.

How many did you find? _____

To the Teacher: Review the picture names with students.
(nurse, necklace, newspaper, nuts, basket, picture)

N n
nest

Listening for initial n

Listen for the Sound

OX

Color the ones that begin like **ox**.

To the Teacher: Review the picture names with students.
(apple, octopus, olives, otter, horse, ostrich)

Listening for initial short o

Name _____

Glue the pictures that begin with a **short o** under the ox.
Glue the other pictures under 😞.

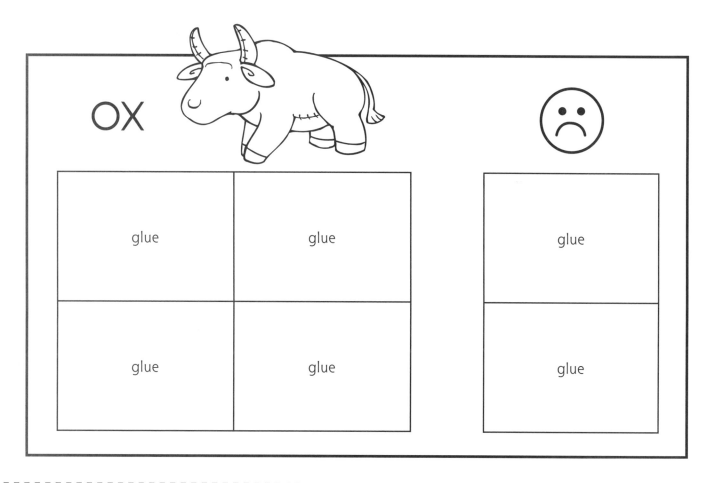

OX

| glue | glue |
| glue | glue |

😞

| glue |
| glue |

Listening for initial short o

Sound-Symbol Association 217

Name _____

What Do You See?

Color the things that begin like **ox**.

OX

How many did you find? _____

To the Teacher: Review the picture names with students.
(octopus, olives, ocean, clouds, sunglasses, hat)

Listening for initial short o

Name _____

P p
pig

Color the ones that begin like **pig**.

To the Teacher: Review the picture names with students.
(pencil, bug, peanut, chick, pin, pumpkin)

Listening for initial p

Cut and Sort

Glue the pictures that begin with **p** under the pig.
Glue the other pictures under 😞.

pig

glue	glue
glue	glue

😞

glue
glue

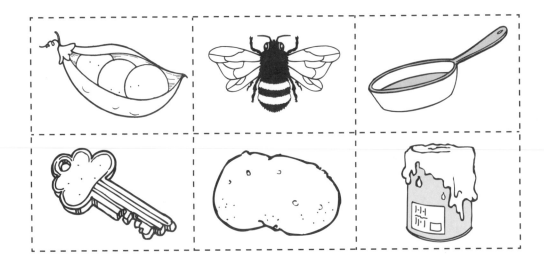

Listening for initial p

Name _____

What Do You See?

Color the things that begin like **pig**.

Pumpkins
10¢ lb.

Pp
pig

How many did you find? _____

To the Teacher: Review the picture names with students.
(parrot, pumpkin, pencil, paper, scale, sign)

Listening for initial p

Listen for the Sound

Qq
queen

Color the ones that begin like **queen**.

To the Teacher: Review the picture names with students.
(quarter, hat, 1/4, quail, girl, quilt)

Listening for initial q

Name _____

Cut and Sort

Glue the pictures that begin with **q** under the queen.
Glue the other pictures under 😞.

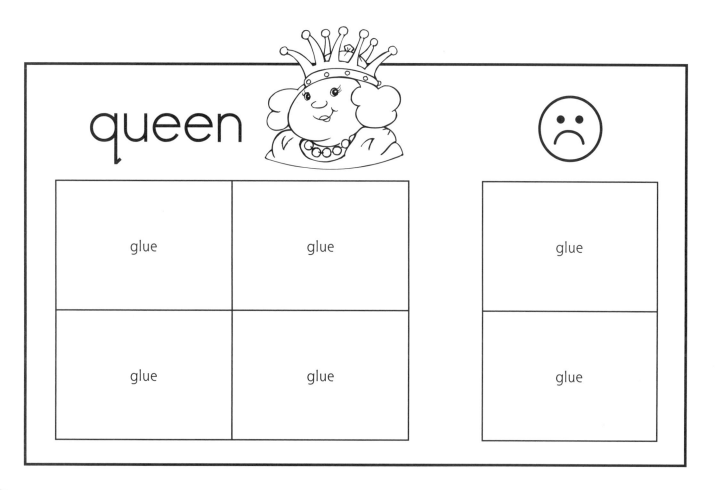

Name _____

Color the things that begin like **queen**.

Qq
queen

How many did you find? _____

To the Teacher: Review the picture names with students.
(quilt, quail, question marks, needle, thread)
Listening for initial q

Name

Listen for the Sound

R r
robot

Color the ones that begin like **robot**.

To the Teacher: Review the picture names with students.
(ring, rainbow, rose, hammer, rabbit)

Listening for initial r

Name

Glue the pictures that begin with **r** under the robot.
Glue the other pictures under 🙁.

robot

glue	glue
glue	glue

glue
glue

Listening for initial r

Name _____

Color the things that begin like **robot**.

How many did you find? _____

To the Teacher: Review the picture names with students.
(rainbow, rabbit, radio, rain, clouds, music)

Rr
robot

Listening for initial r

Name _____

S s
sun

Color the ones that begin like **sun**.

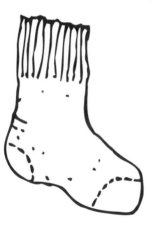

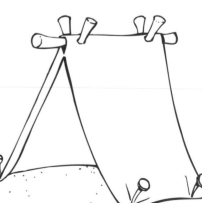

To the Teacher: Review the picture names with students.
(sock, saddle, jeans, tent, soap, saw)

Listening for initial s

Basic Phonics Skills, Level A • EMC 3318 • ©2004 by Evan-Moor Corp.

Name _____

Glue the pictures that begin with **s** under the sun.
Glue the other pictures under 😦.

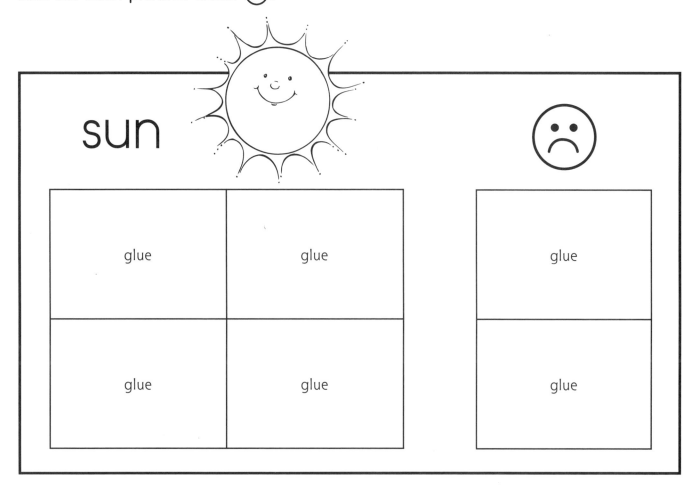

sun

😦

glue	glue
glue	glue

glue
glue

Listening for initial s

Name _____

Color the things that begin like **sun**.

Ss
sun

How many did you find? _____

To the Teacher: Review the picture names with students.
(sailor, sailboat, seagull, squirrel, water, flag)
Listening for initial s

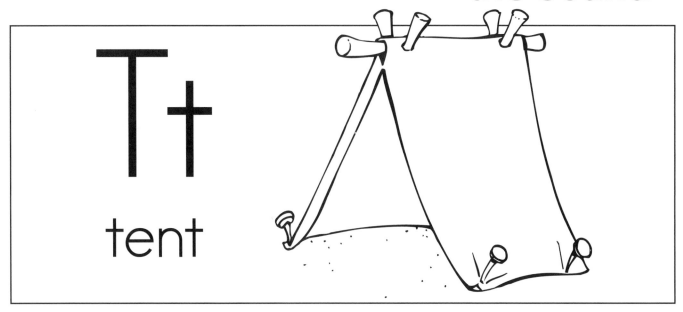

T t
tent

Color the ones that begin like **tent**.

To the Teacher: Review the picture names with students.
(towel, net, turtle, tie, table, jet)

Listening for initial t

Name _____

Glue the pictures that begin with **t** under the tent.
Glue the other pictures under ☹.

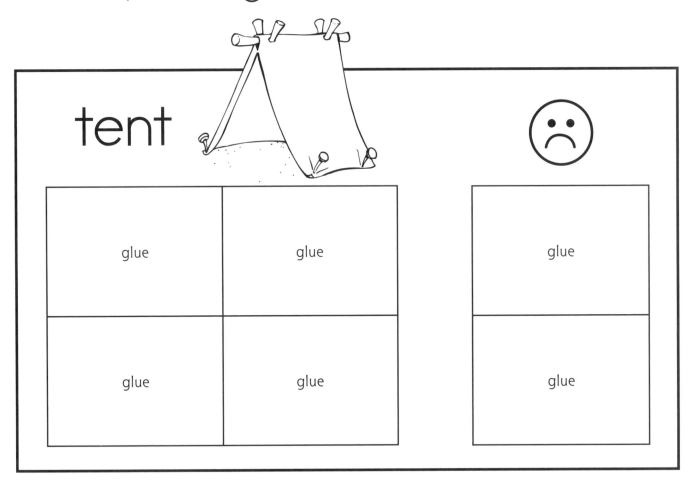

tent

glue	glue
glue	glue

☹

glue
glue

Listening for initial t

Basic Phonics Skills, Level A • EMC 3318 • ©2004 by Evan-Moor Corp.

Name _____

Color the things that begin like **tent**.

T t
tent

How many did you find? _____

To the Teacher: Review the picture names with students.
(tiger, telephone, turtle, ten, flower, frame)

Listening for initial t

Name _____

U u
up

Color the ones that begin like **up**.

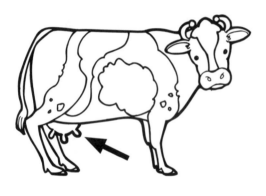

To the Teacher: Review the picture names with students.
(udder, house, umpire, umbrella, tulip, under)

Listening for initial short u

Name _____

Cut and Sort

Glue the pictures that begin with a **short u** under **up**.
Glue the other pictures under 😟 .

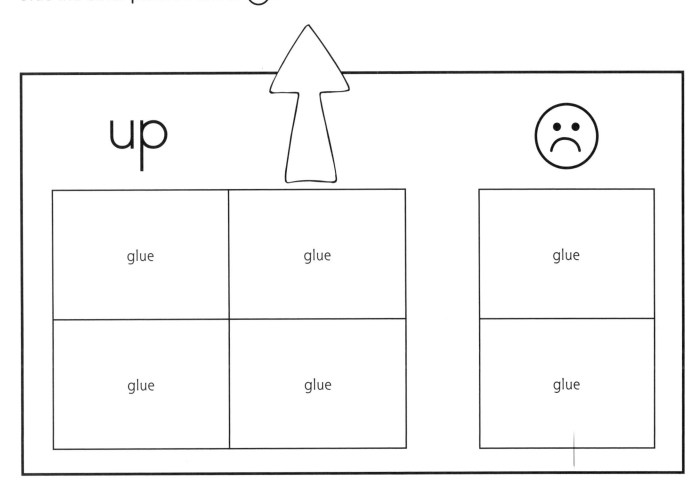

Name

Color the things that begin like **up**.

Uu
up

How many did you find? _____

To the Teacher: Review the picture names with students.
(umpire, umbrella, upside down, base, grass)

Listening for initial short u

Name _____

V v
van

Color the ones that begin like **van**.

To the Teacher: Review the picture names with students.
(valentine, fan, violin, vase, rooster, vacuum)

Name _____

Glue the pictures that begin with a **v** under the van.
Glue the other pictures under 😞 .

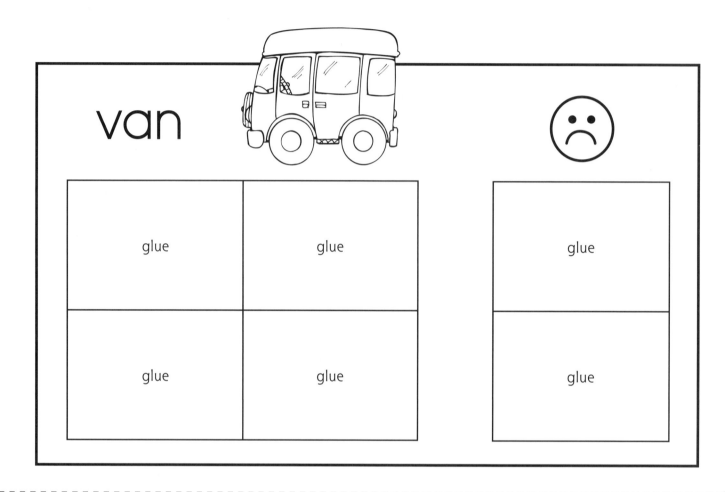

glue	glue	glue
glue	glue	glue

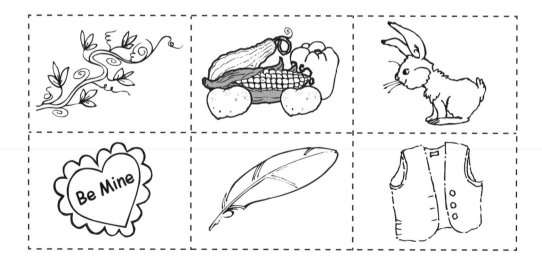

Listening for initial v

Name _

What Do You See?

Color the things that begin like **van**.

How many did you find? _____

To the Teacher: Review the picture names with students.
(vulture, volcano, violin, valentine, tree, cloud)

V v
van

Listening for initial v

Name

W w
wagon

Color the ones that begin like **wagon**.

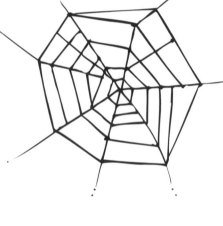

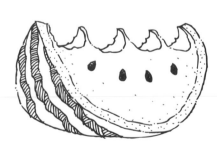

To the Teacher: Review the picture names with students.
(walrus, raccoon, web, umbrella, watermelon, wave)

Listening for initial w

Name _____

Cut and Sort

Glue the pictures that begin with **w** under the wagon.
Glue the other pictures under 🙁 .

wagon

glue	glue
glue	glue

glue
glue

Name _____

What Do You See?

Color the things that begin like **wagon**.

Ww
wagon

How many did you find? _____

To the Teacher: Review the picture names with students.
(walrus, watch, watermelon, water, sun)

Listening for initial w

242 **Sound-Symbol Association**   Basic Phonics Skills, Level A • EMC 3318 • ©2004 by Evan-Moor Corp.

Name _____

X x
fox

Color the ones that end like **fox**.

To the Teacher: Review the picture names with students of things that end like *fox*. (ax, ox, frog, box, dog)

Listening for the ending x

Sound-Symbol Association

Cut and Sort

Glue the pictures that end with **x** under the fox.
Glue the other pictures under 😦 .

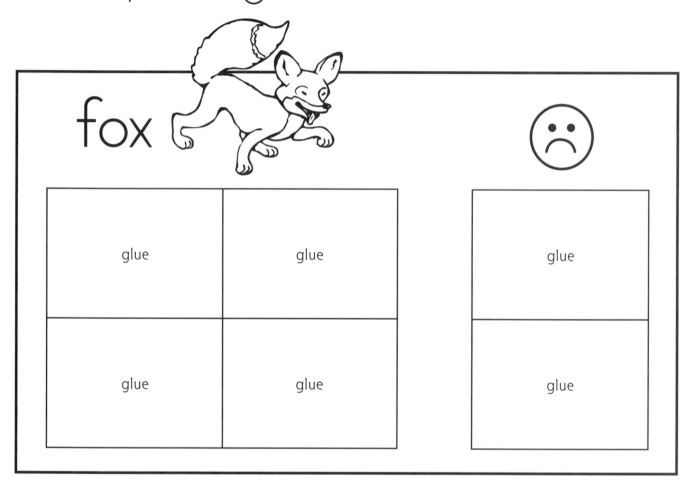

fox

glue	glue		glue
glue	glue		glue

Listening for the ending x

Basic Phonics Skills, Level A • EMC 3318 • ©2004 by Evan-Moor Corp.

Name _____

What Do You See?

X is hiding.
Circle **X** where you find it.

How many did you find? _____

Xx
X ray

Visual perception

©2004 by Evan-Moor Corp. • Basic Phonics Skills, Level A • EMC 3318

Listen for the Sound

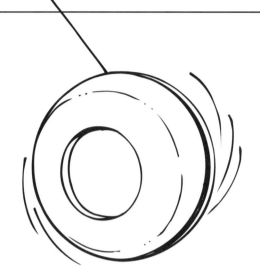

Y y
yo-yo

Color the ones that begin like **yo-yo**.

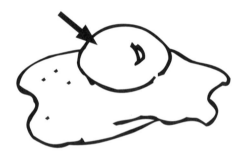

To the Teacher: Review the picture names with students.
(yak, yolk, horse, yarn, nickel, yogurt)

Listening for initial y

Name _____

Glue the pictures that begin with **y** under the yo-yo.
Glue the other pictures under 🙁 .

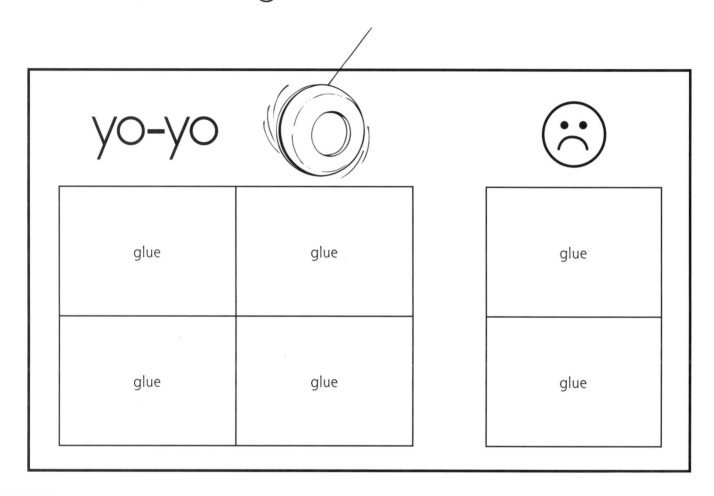

Name _____

What Do You See?

Color the things that begin like **yo-yo**.

How many did you find? _____

To the Teacher: Review the picture names with students.
(yak, yarn, yogurt, rocking chair, table)
Listening for initial y

Yy
yo-yo

Basic Phonics Skills, Level A • EMC 3318 • ©2004 by Evan-Moor Corp.

Listen for the Sound

Z z
zebra

Color the ones that begin like **zebra**.

To the Teacher: Review the picture names with students.
(zero, zigzag, zipper, bees, sailboat, zinnia)

Listening for initial z

Sound-Symbol Association 249

Name _____

Glue the pictures that begin with **z** under the zebra.
Glue the other pictures under 😞.

Listening for initial z

Name _____

What Do You See?

Color the things that begin like **zebra**.

How many did you find? _____

To the Teacher: Review the picture names with students.
(zipper, zoo, zigzag, giraffe, boy, elephant, monkey)

Zz
zebra

Listening for initial z

Sound-Symbol Association 251

Little Alphabet Readers

green apple

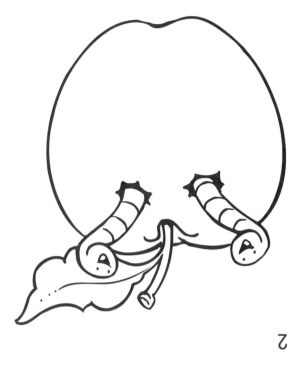

2

red apple

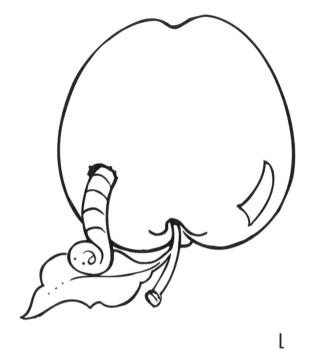

1

fold 2

fold 1

fold 1

3

yellow apple

Aa

apple

little bats

big bat

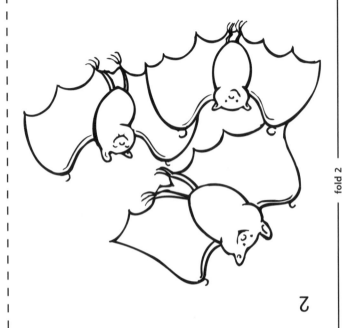

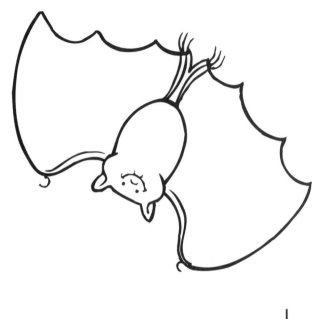

fold 2

2

1

fold 1

fold 1

3

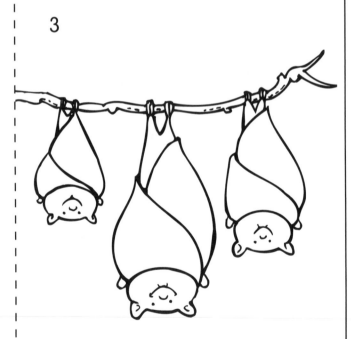

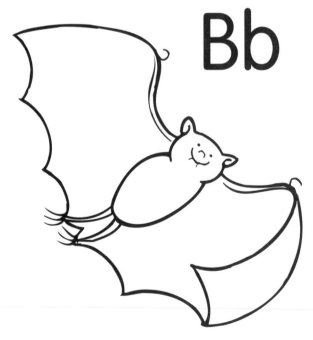

Bb

big and little bats

bat

  Basic Phonics Skills, Level A • EMC 3318 • ©2004 by Evan-Moor Corp.

¿Cake?

¿Cake?

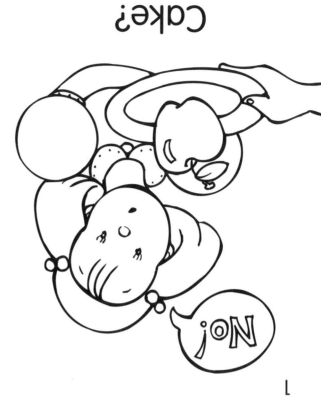

2

fold 2

1

fold 1 ⸺ ⸺ fold 1

3

Cake?

Cc

cake

2 ducks

1 duck

fold 2

2

1

fold 1

fold 1

3

Dd

3 ducks

duck

brown egg

2

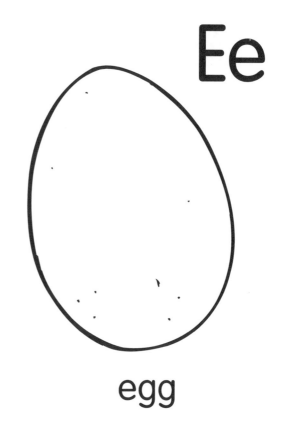

blue egg

fold 2

1

fold 1 — — fold 1

3

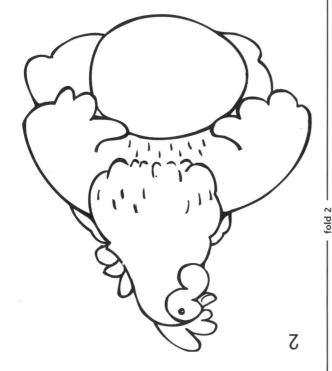

pink egg

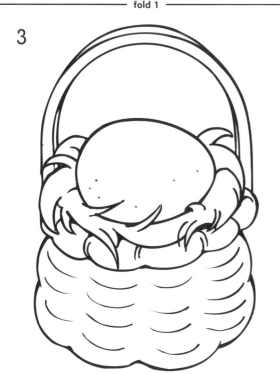

Ee

egg

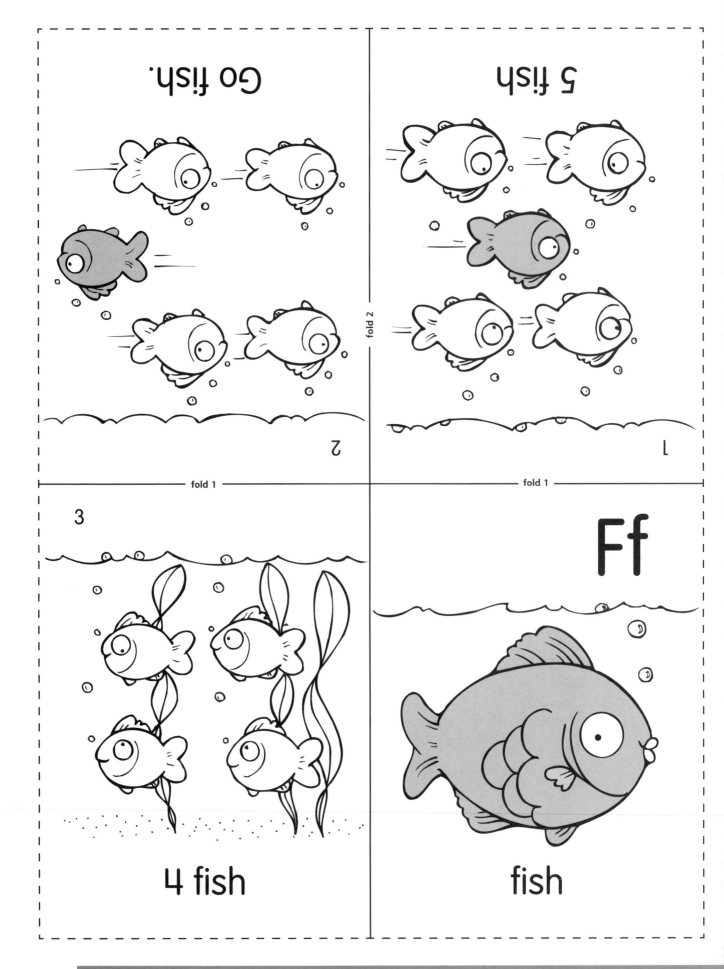

Go fish.

5 fish

2

1

fold 2

fold 1

fold 1

3

Ff

4 fish

fish

Basic Phonics Skills, Level A • EMC 3318 • ©2004 by Evan-Moor Corp.

Go, go!

Go, goat.

2

1

fold 2

fold 1 — fold 1

3

Gg

Good goat.

goat

Hen has eggs.

fold 2

2

One hen.

1

fold 1

fold 1

3

Hen has chicks.

Hh

hen

LITTLE ALPHABET READERS Basic Phonics Skills, Level A • EMC 3318 • ©2004 by Evan-Moor Corp.

little igloo

big igloo

fold 2

2

1

fold 1

fold 1

3

Ii

Iggie's igloo

igloo

Go, jeep.

1

fold 2

Go, jeep.

2

fold 1

fold 1

3

whee!

Go, jeep, go!

Jj

jeep

 Basic Phonics Skills, Level A • EMC 3318 • ©2004 by Evan-Moor Corp.

2 koalas

1 koala

3 koalas

Kk

koala

yellow leaf

2

red leaf

1

fold 2

fold 1   fold 1

3

Look! Look!

Ll

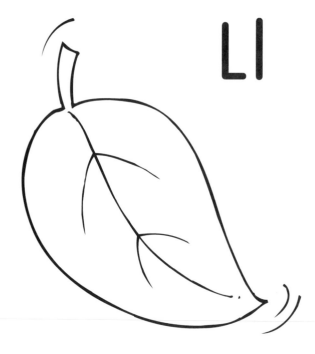

leaf

Basic Phonics Skills, Level A • EMC 3318 • ©2004 by Evan-Moor Corp.

Moon?

2

See the moon.

1

fold 2

fold 1

fold 1

3

See the moon!

Mm

moon

2 in a nest

2

1 in a nest

fold 2

1

fold 1

fold 1

3

Yum!

Nn

nest

Basic Phonics Skills, Level A • EMC 3318 • ©2004 by Evan-Moor Corp.

fox in a box

2

ox in a box

1

3

Ox and fox
in a box.

Oo

ox

Pig is not pink.

2

Pig is pink.

1

fold 2

fold 1

fold 1

3

Pig is pink again.

Pp

pig

Basic Phonics Skills, Level A • EMC 3318 • ©2004 by Evan-Moor Corp.

See the queen bee.

2

See the queen.

1

fold 2

fold 1

fold 1

3

See me.

Qq

queen

Fix robot.

Sad robot.

2

1

fold 2

fold 1

fold 1

3

Go, robot!

Rr

robot

 Basic Phonics Skills, Level A • EMC 3318 • ©2004 by Evan-Moor Corp.

No sun.

2

Sun!

3

Sun!

Sun!

1

Ss

sun

2 in a tent

1 in a tent

fold 2

2

1

fold 1

fold 1

3

Tt

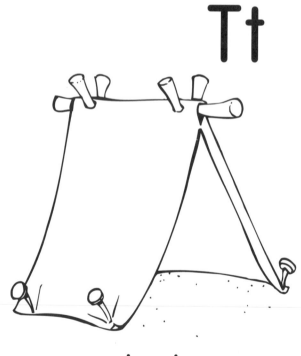

3 in a tent

tent

Up, up, up.

Up.

2

1

fold 2

fold 1

fold 1

3

Up is fun.

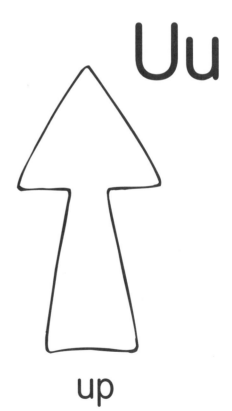

Uu

up

See the van go.

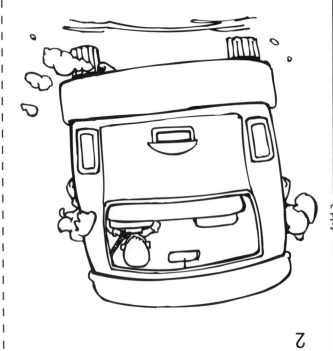

2

Get in the van.

1

3

DOG
SHOW

See the van stop.

Vv

van

 Basic Phonics Skills, Level A • EMC 3318 • ©2004 by Evan-Moor Corp.

2 in a wagon

1 in a wagon

3 in a wagon

Ww

wagon

See Tab's X ray.

See Sam's X ray.

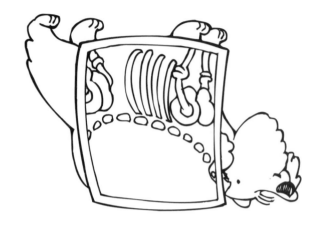

2

1

fold 2

fold 1

fold 1

3

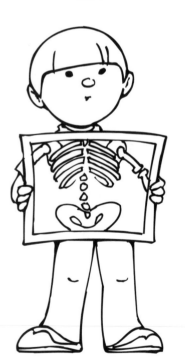

Xx

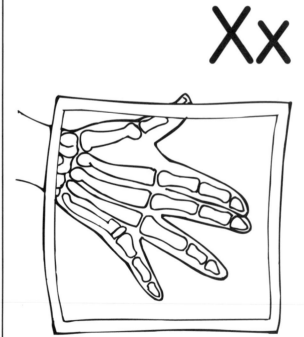

See Pat's X ray.

X ray

fold 2

Yo-yo up.

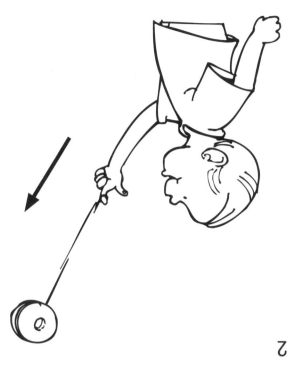

2

See the yo-yo.

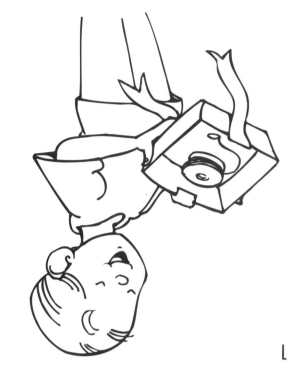

1

fold 1

fold 1

3

Yo-yo down.

Yy

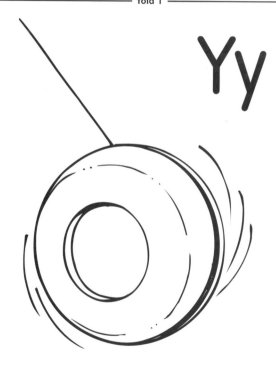

yo-yo

Zebra zags.

Zebra zigs.

2

1

fold 2

fold 1

fold 1

3

Zz

Zebra zigzags
at the zoo.

zebra

Basic Phonics Skills, Level A • EMC 3318 • ©2004 by Evan-Moor Corp.

Answer Key

Page 8 Circled: 2, 3, 5, 6

Page 9 Matched: open-closed; on-off; up-down

Page 10 Left hand yellow, right hand red; left mitten and right glove circled

Page 11 Traced from left to right

Page 12 Traced from left to right

Page 13 **Red:** top button, scoop, mug, towel;
Blue: bottom button, scoop, mug, towel

Page 14 Traced from top to bottom

Page 15 Traced from top to bottom

Page 16 Colored: 1, 4, 5, 6

Page 17 Colored: 1, 2, 4, 5

Page 18 Objects matched

Page 19 Objects matched

Page 20 Shapes drawn

Page 21 Matching shapes colored

Page 22 Colored: last bow, first tree, second candle, third turtle

Page 23 Colored: third cup, second plate, second monkey, last door

Page 24 Drawn: 1. tendril; 2. buttonholes; 3. nose; 4. windowpanes; 5. wheel; 6. hour hand

Page 25 Matching letters circled

Page 26 Drawn: 1. seam lines; 2. pole; 3. O; 4. top line of the T; 5. eyebrow; 6. drumstick

Page 27 First object colored; first object drawn

Page 28 Objects at end colored; first objects circled; objects drawn at end

Page 29 First objects circled, middle objects colored, and last objects crossed out

Page 30 Missing pictures drawn

Page 31 Six objects circled

Page 32 Five objects circled

Page 33 Five letters circled

Page 34 Five letters circled

Page 35 Circled: third candy cane, second boy, last dog, first mug

Page 36 Circled: last flag, third boot, second hook, second worm

Page 37 Circled: shoes, clock, fish, gingerbread man, hammer, boot

Page 38 Circled: sun, snowman, socks, ice-cream cones, skates on snake, frog/bubbles, puddle

Page 39 Colored: 1. ring and necklace; 2. ball and cap; 3. crayon and pen; 4. both leaves

Page 40 Circled: 1, 2, 3, 6, 7, 8

Page 41 Matched: cat–dish, fish–fishbowl, spoon–fork, lamp–light bulb

Page 42 Matched: baby–rattle, train–track, lock–key, plant–flower pot

Page 43 X'd out: cat, shirt, hook, spoon

Page 44 X'd out: tree, scissors, butterfly, bell

Page 45 Answers will vary, but should match category.

Page 46 All words should be circled.

Page 48 1: star, fish, house; **2:** apple, table, baby

Basic Phonics Skills, Level A • EMC 3318 • ©2004 by Evan-Moor Corp.

Page 49

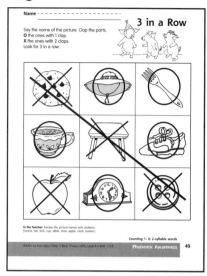

Page 50 1: star, top, car, lamp, hand; **2:** baby, hammer, apple, mitten

Page 51 1: shoe, box, spoon; **2:** carrots, arrow, flower

Page 52 1 circled: 1, 2, 4, 6, 8; **2 circled:** 3, 5, 7, 9

Page 53 1: dog, bear; **2:** rooster, monkey; **3:** elephant, butterfly

Page 54 1 circled: 1, 3, 7; **2 circled:** 4, 6, 8; **3 circled:** 2, 5, 9

Page 55 1: hand, frog; **2:** rabbit, wagon, lettuce; **3:** butterfly, elephant, ladybug

Page 56 Colored: hat, bat, mat, rat

Page 57 Circled: 1. cat, hat; 2. hat, mat, bat; 3. bat, rat

Page 58 Rhyme: 2, 3; **Do not rhyme:** 1, 4

Page 59 Colored: rake, snowflake, snake, lake

Page 60 Circled: 1. steak, rake; 2. shake, snake; 3. snowflake, lake

Page 61 Rhyme: 1, 3; **Do not rhyme:** 2, 4

Page 62 Cake: snake, lake, rake; **Cat:** rat, hat, mat

Page 63 Colored: lip, rip, whip

Page 64 Circled: 1. lip, rip; 2. ship, drip; 3. cake, rake; 4. hat, bat

Page 65 Rhyme: 2, 3; **Do not rhyme:** 1, 4

Page 66 Colored: light, night, write, bite

Page 67 Circled: 1. knight, light; 2. bite, night; 3. lip, ship; 4. rake, snake

Page 68 Rhyme: 1, 3, 4; **Do not rhyme:** 2

Page 69 Ship: zip, drip, lip; **Kite:** light, bite, night

Page 70 Colored: note, coat, boat, float

Page 71 Circled: 1. goat, note; 2. boat, float; 3. cake, lake; 4. night, light

Page 72 Rhyme: 4; **Do not rhyme:** 1, 2, 3

Page 73 Colored: mop, stop, hop

Page 74 Circled: 1. top, hop; 2. mop, pop; 3. soap, rope; 4. zip, ship

Page 75 Rhyme: 2. 4; **Do not rhyme:** 1, 3

Page 76 Top: mop, stop, hop; **Goat:** boat, note, coat

Page 77 Colored: red, thread, sled, bread

Page 78 Circled: 1. red, sled; 2. mop, hop; 3. thread, bed; 4. soap, rope

Page 79 Colored: sheep, sweep, sleep

Page 80 Circled: 1. sleep, sweep; 2. sheep, peep; 3. red, bed; 4. mop, top

Page 81 Rhyme: 1, 4; **Do not rhyme:** 2, 3

Page 82 Jeep: sheep, beep, sleep; **Bed:** sled, thread, red

Page 83 Colored: rug, hug, mug, jug

Page 84 Circled: 1. rug, bug; 2. hug, mug; 3. mug, plug; 4. bug, mug

Page 85 Rhyme: 1, 4; **Do not rhyme:** 2, 3

 Basic Phonics Skills, Level A • EMC 3318 • ©2004 by Evan-Moor Corp.

Page 86 Colored: thumb, plum, gum

Page 87 Circled: 1. thumb, gum; 2. plum, hum; 3. drum, plum; 4. sheep, sweep

Page 88 **Rhyme:** 1, 3; **Do not rhyme:** 2, 4

Page 89 **Drum:** gum, plum, thumb; **Bug:** rug, hug, jug

Page 90 Colored: tack, sack, black, backpack

Page 91 Circled: 1. back, stack; 2. track, crack; 3. black, sack; 4. tacks, tracks

Page 92 **Rhyme:** 3, 4: **Do not rhyme:** 1, 2

Page 93 Colored: stick, lick, kick, brick

Page 94 Circled: 1. lick, stick; 2. chick, pick; 3. brick, kick; 4. sack, track

Page 95 **Rhyme:** 1, 4; **Do not rhyme:** 2, 3

Page 96 **Chick:** stick, kick, brick; **Track:** sack, tack, black

Page 97 Colored: clock, sock, block, rock

Page 98 Circled: 1. sock, block; 2. lock, rock; 3. clock, sock; 4. block, tock

Page 99 **Rhyme:** 1, 4; **Do not rhyme:** 2, 3

Page 100 **Sock:** lock, block, rock; **Brick:** stick, kick, chick

Page 101 Circled: 1. cake, car; 2. mouse, man; 3. soap, scissors; 4. bed, bike

Page 102 Circled: 1. gum, gate; 2. lemon, lips; 3. paint, pen; 4. ten, tub

Page 103 All begin with the same sound except number 3.

Page 104 Matched: 1. vest–van; 2. 9–nest; 3. bird–barn; 4. goat–gopher; 5. yarn–yo-yo

Page 105 Circled: 1. crib, bib; 2. foot, boat; 3. jam, broom; 4. brick, hook

Page 106 Circled: 1. pig, bug; 2. ball, girl; 3. fan, sun; 4. kiss, gas

Page 107 All end with the same sound except number 1.

Page 108 Matched: 1. wig–rug; 2. 10–pan; 3. tub–crab; 4. gum–jam; 5. bat–mitt

Page 109 Circles filled in: 1. 3; 2. 2; 3. 4; 4. 3; 5. 4; 6. 3

Page 110 Circles filled in: 1. 3; 2. 2; 3. 3; 4. 2; 5. 3; 6. 3

Page 111 Numbers circled: 1. 3; 2. 3; 3. 3; 4. 2; 5. 4; 6. 3

Page 112 Numbers circled: 1. 2; 2. 3; 3. 4; 4. 4; 5. 3; 6. 3

Pages 116 and 117 Students write and identify A and a.

Pages 118 and 119 Students write and match B and b.

Pages 120 and 121 Students write and match C and c.

Pages 122 and 123 Students write and identify D and d.

Pages 124 and 125 Students write and match E and e.

Pages 126 and 127 Students write and match F and f.

Pages 128 and 129 Students write and identify G and g.

Pages 130 and 131 Students write and identify H and h.

Pages 132 and 133 Students write and match I and i.

Pages 134 and 135 Students write and match J and j.

Pages 136 and 137 Students write and identify K and k.

Pages 138 and 139 Students write and match L and l.

Pages 140 and 141 Students write and identify M and m.

Pages 142 and 143 Students write and match N and n.

Pages 144 and 145 Students write and identify O and o.

Pages 146 and 147 Students write and match P and p.

Pages 148 and 149 Students write and identify Q and q.

Pages 150 and 151 Students write and match R and r.

 Basic Phonics Skills, Level A • EMC 3318 • ©2004 by Evan-Moor Corp.

Pages 152 and 153 Students write and identify S and s.

Pages 154 and 155 Students write and match T and t.

Pages 156 and 157 Students write and match U and u.

Pages 158 and 159 Students write and identify V and v.

Pages 160 and 161 Students write and match W and w.

Pages 162 and 163 Students write and identify X and x.

Pages 164 and 165 Students write and match Y and y.

Pages 166 and 167 Students write and identify Z and z.

Pages 168 and 169 Students write the missing capital letters.

Pages 170 and 171 Students write the missing lowercase letters.

Page 172 Students write the words and then fill in the missing letters: C, G, U, m, p, f.

Page 174 Colored: ant, anchor, ax, antlers

Page 175 Apple: anchor, ax, antlers, ant

Page 176 Colored: apple, ant, antlers

Page 177 Colored: balloon, butterfly, bus, ball

Page 178 Bat: bag, boat, book, basket

Page 179 Colored: balloon, bear, bow tie, butterfly, ball

Page 180 Colored: cookie, cup, camera, cap

Page 181 Cake: cat, can, car, candle

Page 182 Colored: clock, candle, cat, cane

Page 183 Colored: doll, dime, door, dog

Page 184 Duck: dishes, dime, dollar, desk

Page 185 Colored: dog, door, daffodil

Page 186 Colored: elf, Eskimo, envelope

Page 187 Egg: elf, envelope, elephant, Eskimo

Page 188 Colored: elephant, envelope, Eskimo

Page 189 Colored: 4, feather, fence, fan

Page 190 Fish: finger, flag, feather, fork

Page 191 Colored, fox, flower, fence, feather

Page 192 Colored: gate, gift, guitar, garbage can

Page 193 Goat: girl, gopher, grapes, glove

Page 194 Colored: gorilla, guitar, goose, grass

Page 195 Colored: house, hose, hand, heart

Page 196 Hen: hammer, hot dog, hamburger, helicopter

Page 197 Colored: horse, hat, hearts, hose

Page 198 Colored: inch, insects, instruments

Page 199 Igloo: inch, insects, Indians, ink

Page 200 Colored: insects, ink, inchworm

Page 201 Colored: jelly beans, jet, jump rope, jam

Page 202 Jeep: jet, jacks, jam, jug

Page 203 Colored: jack-in-the-box, jelly beans, jump rope, jar

Page 204 Colored: kangaroo, kite, key, king

Page 205 Koala: kite, key, kiss, kick

Page 206 Colored: kite, king, kangaroo, kiwi

Page 207 Colored: log, lemon, ladder, lion

Page 208 Leaf: lip, lemon, lake, log

Page 209 Colored: lamb, lion, ladder, ladybug

Page 210 Colored: mitt, monkey, mop, mouse

Page 211 **Moon:** map, mouse, mirror, mittens

Page 212 Colored: monkey, mop, mouse

Page 213 Colored: nest, necklace, nickel, net

Page 214 **Nest:** nose, nickel, nut, needle

Page 215 Colored: nurse, necklace, newspaper, nuts

Page 216 Colored: octopus, olives, otter, ostrich

Page 217 **Ox:** otter, on, olives, octopus

Page 218 Colored: octopus, olives

Page 219 Colored: pencil, peanut, pin, pumpkin

Page 220 Pig: peas, pan, potato, paint

Page 221 Colored: pumpkin, parrot, pencil, paper

Page 222 Colored: quarter, one-quarter, quail, quilt

Page 223 Queen: quack, question mark, quarter, quail

Page 224 Colored: quail, quilt, question marks

Page 225 Colored: ring, rainbow, rose, rabbit

Page 226 Robot: rope, ruler, rooster, roof

Page 227 Colored: rainbow, rabbit, radio, rain

Page 228 Colored: sock, saddle, soap, saw

Page 229 Sun: saw, salt, soap, sad

Page 230 Colored: sailboat, sailor, squirrel, seagull

Page 231 Colored: towel, turtle, tie, table

Page 232 Tent: telephone, 10, tape, table

Page 233 Colored: tiger, telephone, 10, turtle

Page 234 Colored: udder, umpire, under, umbrella

Page 235 Up: udder, umpire, umbrella, under

Page 236 Colored: umpire, umbrella, upside down

Page 237 Colored: valentine, violin, vase, vacuum

Page 238 Van: vine, vegetables, valentine, vest

Page 239 Colored: volcano, vulture, violin, valentine

Page 240 Colored: walrus, web, watermelon, wave

Page 241 Wagon: web, walrus, wig, watch

Page 242 Colored: walrus, watermelon, watch, water

Page 243 Colored: ax, ox, box

Page 244 Fox: ox, 6, box, ax

Page 245 5 X's should be circled

Page 246 Colored: yak, yolk, yarn, yogurt

Page 247 Yo-yo: yes, yolk, yarn, yawn

Page 248 Colored: yak, yarn, yogurt

Page 249 Colored: zero, zigzag, zipper, zinnia

Page 250 Zebra: zigzag, zebra, zero, zipper

Page 251 Colored: zoo, zipper, zigzag

Basic Phonics Skills, Level A • EMC 3318 • ©2004 by Evan-Moor Corp.